SPONTANEOUS RECOGNITION

Discussions with

SWAMI SHAMBHAVANANDA

Edited by Ashok N. Srivastava, Ph.D.

A Publication of SGRY

Published by SGRY
PO Box 307
Eldorado Springs, CO 80025
U.S.A
email: eldo@rmii.com

Edited by Ashok N. Srivastava, Ph.D.

First published in 1995
Revised edition 1998

ISBN 1-888386-01-0

Library of Congress Catalog Card Number: 98-87503

Library of Congress Cataloging-in-Publication Data

Shambhavananda, Swami, 1947
Spontaneous Recognition : Discussions with Swami Shambhavananda / by Swami Shambhavananda. – 2nd ed.

ISBN 1-888386-01-0

1. Philosophy 2. Religion 1. Title

Printed in Canada

To my teachers:

Swami Nityananda

Swami Muktananda

Swami Rudrananda

Sri Nityananda, root Guru of the Shambhavananda lineage

CONTENTS

Swami Shambhavananda (Swamiji)

Swami Shambhavananda and the Shambhava School of Yoga

Born on the fall equinox in 1947, Shambhavananda is the son of Italian dairy farmers. The family also grew vegetables which they sold from their truck in the summer and his mother worked at a factory to supplement the family income. When he was a baby, his mother had a small statue of a Buddha which she kept near his crib. Everyday she burned incense and placed it before the statue. As a Christian, she was never quite sure why, but later said that she thought that is why he became a yogi.

As a boy, Swamiji helped his dad and older brothers milk the cows by hand before heading off to school in the mornings. He had a recurring vision on the farm of an unusual being floating in the air. It wasn't until many years later that he recognized the vision as Padmasambhava, the master Yogi who brought Buddhism to Tibet. He also felt a calling to be a spiritual minister (he thought). One day when the calling felt particularly strong, he asked aloud to the sky, "Should I become a minister?" He heard a very distinct Brooklyn Jewish voice say, "Not yet." He heard that voice again when he met his Guru.

In the '60s, he became involved with the hippie life-style, while looking for a new awareness and direction both for himself and the country. It was in the late '60s that he met his

Swami Rudrananda (Rudi)

Guru, Swami Rudrananda (Rudi). It was the turning point in his life. Rudi affected him profoundly. He received a deep spiritual transmission from Rudi that altered the way he perceived everything. It awakened a vast spiritual yearning within him and began his life of dedication to yoga and meditation – the calling of his childhood.

Under Rudi's guidance, he began teaching Kundalini meditation and Rudi suggested that he start an Ashram for him in Italy. Instead, Shambhavananda stayed on to help with the Ashram in Indiana. After Rudi's Mahasamadhi (final liberation at the time of death) and several years of service to the Indiana Ashram, Swamiji was ready to start a center. With a small group of students, he headed for Boulder, Colorado, and in the summer of 1975 began his own work and Ashram.

He taught as Rudi taught him while slowly sinking in his roots. The little Sangha grew over the years, with many people passing through its doors. Within a few years, a large old house surrounded by fraternities on University Hill was purchased. It was a noisy, lustful area which gave aspiring Yogis many a challenge to their contemplative practice. Swamiji says it is through this experience that he earned Eldorado Mountain Ashram. The Ashram is nestled on a ridge overlooking a spectacularly beautiful view of Eldorado Canyon. It is surrounded by state parks and quiet neighbors.

About ten years after Rudi's death, Swamiji was visiting the Mahasamadhi shrine of Rudi's Guru, Swami Nityananda, in Ganeshpuri, India. It is an extraordinary place where you can still feel the living vibration of this great Maha Siddha (Master Yogi). Swamiji had visited the Mahasamadhi shrine before, but on this particular trip he decided to also visit the Ashram of another of Nityananda's spiritual sons, Swami Muktananda (affectionately called Baba). Baba was in the U.S. at the time. When entering the meditation area and personal meditation cave of Muktananda, Swamiji was struck by the enormous quantity of Shakti (spiritual energy). He knew this was the abode of a remarkable yogi and he also knew, "I must meet him."

Swami Muktananda (affectionately called Baba)

After returning to the States, he discovered Baba was teaching in Florida, and he made plans to visit him. Rudi had also studied with Baba for 14 years. Swamiji was aware of the tumultuous nature of the relationship between Baba and Rudi and expected to be treated with a tough and heavy hand.

Instead, Baba treated him like a long-lost son, showering him with love and affection. Swamiji hardly knew how to react. He said, for the first week after meeting Baba, all he did was cry. He felt the years of hardship and struggle from working on his own melt away.

Baba was incredibly gracious, loving and supportive. He told Swamiji, "You have very good Shakti. You should keep doing what you're doing. You're doing good work. Someday you will have a big place. You will give Shakti to many people and help many people." He went on to say, "You don't need to join Siddha Yoga (the name of Baba's international meditation school). Your relationship is with me." Finally he told him, "You should understand Buddhism, you should know Buddhism."

After several years, Baba asked Swamiji to become a Swami. Swamiji trusted Baba's guidance and took the initiation. Under Baba and the Mahamandeleshewar (who performed the ceremony), he entered the Saraswati order of Swamis, and Baba gave him the name Shambhavananda. The name means "bliss of the Shiva state or bliss of the natural state of being." Swamiji believes that Baba chose the name Shambhavananda because of his nature. In the Shiva Sutras, the Shambhava Mudra is described as *having one's eyes wide open*, not removed from or isolated from the senses and still remaining immersed in the awareness of Shiva or consciousness. In the Shambhava Mudra, it is not necessary to renounce the physical world in order to remain established in the consciousness of the Self.

After Baba's death in 1982, Swamiji continued about his work as both Rudi and Baba had guided him. In 1987, various Tibetan Lamas began to visit the Ashram. Swamiji hosted them and they gave teachings on the Vajrayana Buddhist way, which is quite similar to Baba's philosophy of Kashmir Shaivism. Now Swamiji understood why Baba had instructed him to learn Buddhism. The sameness and Truth in the two paths became more pronounced than the differences. Rudi also had a strong Tibetan Buddhist connection, and Baba had once told him that he had been a Tibetan Lama in a previous life.

Eldorado Mountain Yoga Ashram continued to grow and flourish, but Swamiji thought it would also be helpful to have a retreat center where aspirants could spend an extended time doing spiritual practice. He thought it should be in a quiet place, far from daily distractions, and that it should be staffed by full-time yoga practitioners. He thought it should be an

Students in progress of building the Shoshoni Temple

environment for discovering the Inner Self. Thus, Shoshoni was born.

Shambhavananda's life work has been in service to God and his Gurus. The form it has taken has been in the building of sanctuaries (ashrams) for spiritual aspirants to practice their sadhana. It is for this reason that Eldorado Mountain Yoga Ashram and Shoshoni Yoga Retreat were created. The feeling

Guests at Shoshoni

of the ashrams is like Swamiji, warm and friendly with sweet, loving people. Guests and visitors come from all over the world to share in the feeling of Sangha (spiritual family).

Shambhavananda Yogi is a radiant, big-hearted teacher who is a master of Kundalini Yoga. He teaches a method for meditation and growth called Shambhava Yoga. His vision for Eldorado and Shoshoni is to create an environment conducive to inner growth, nurturing practitioners toward the realization of their true Self or Buddha nature. The centers provide residential areas for full-time yogis, non-resident classes, and retreat or visitor accommodations. In addition, our Sangha has grown to include ashrams and centers in Adelaide, Australia, and Norwich, England, as well as various centers throughout the U.S.

As old as the hills, in the footsteps of enlightened beings, this is the practice of Shambhava Yoga. Shambhava is the natural state beyond thought and doership. It is to experience everything as Shiva or consciousness. It is a non-dual experience. The finite perception and the infinite are only so in terms of perspective. It is a simple but profound teaching.

Without denying our inherently pure nature, there is the recognition that due to obscurations and karmas we are unable to live in the pure state. For this reason, we use the methods of the great sages, seers, and enlightened beings throughout history, especially mantra repetition or Japa, cultivation of love and devotion for God or the true nature in all, and meditation.

Swami Nityananda was an *Avadhut*, a being of extraordinary detachment from worldly desires, deeply rooted in the essence of consciousness, able to see the same radiant self in all beings (nothing insentient), rising far above the waves of samsara. This Nityananda is the main inspiration to our path. He is the bright lamp which illumines the darkness. He was a being of such extreme brilliance that he continues to shine on those who even look at his picture. Through his contact, many people were profoundly affected. In particular, two whom we revere, Swami Rudrananda and Swami Muktananda, both received Nityananda's transmission or Shaktipata.

Shambhavananda, our living teacher, is rightly described by the name which Baba Muktananda gave to him: Shambhav-ananda, which means the bliss of the natural state. His method of training students of yoga is unencumbered by dogma. He relates to the latent spiritual energy within the aspirant, not to their limited view of themselves. In describing the essence of Nityananda's teachings, Swami Muktananda quotes him as saying, "The heart is the hub of all sacred places. Go there and roam in it." It is this holy place within which Shambhavananda encourages seekers to explore.

– Faith Stone

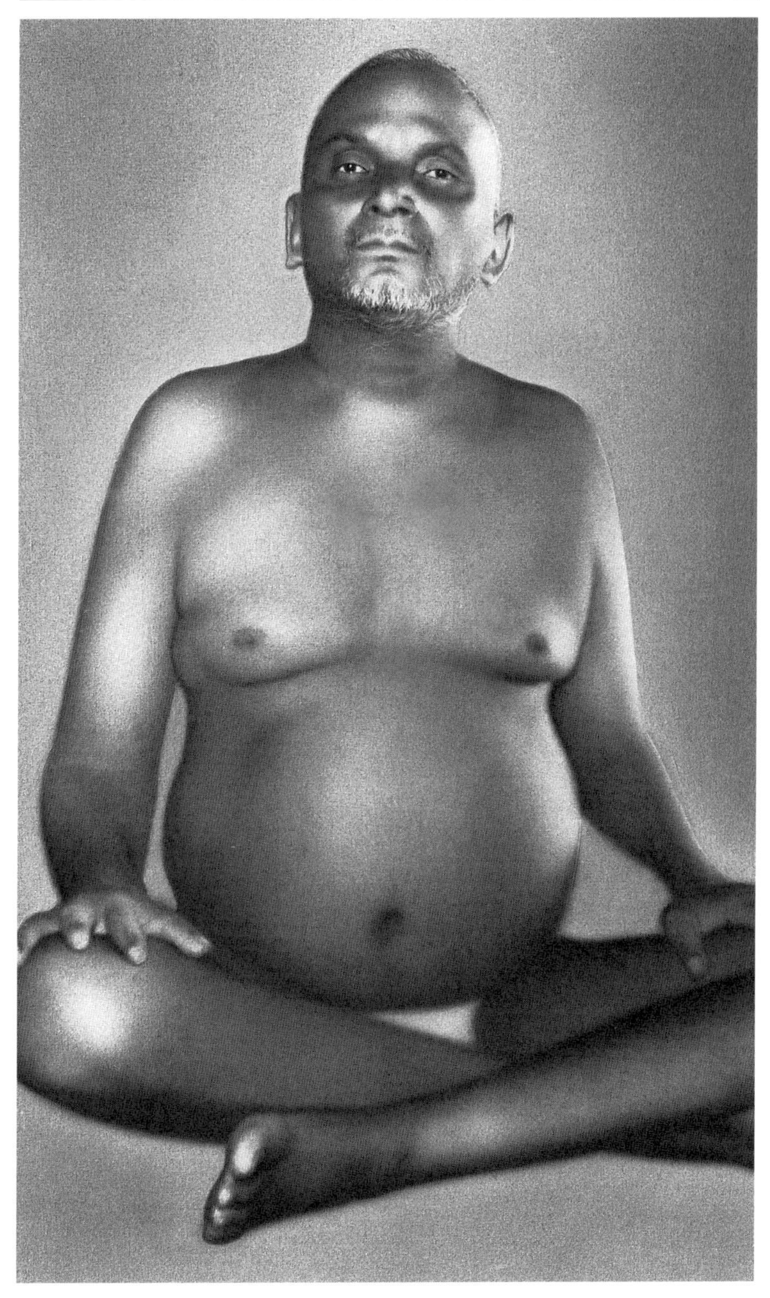

Sri Nityananda, a fully realized Saint

The meditation dome at the Eldorado Mountain Yoga Ashram

Shoshoni Temple

FOREWORD

I don't give lectures; I answer questions. If you have any questions, please feel free to ask.

It was on a brilliant blue summer day that I first visited the Eldorado Mountain Yoga Ashram. I wandered about, admiring the neatness and simplicity of the grounds. I looked through the window of the meditation dome and saw a statue of Swami Nityananda seated at the altar. Nityananda was one of modern India's greatest sages and, as I came to know, the head of the lineage of teachers at the ashram. I walked casually around the dome, admiring the spectacular scenery surrounding this small ashram at the foot of the Rocky Mountains.

Looking east into the distance, I could see the great plains of Colorado, spread golden beneath the sky. Looking west, the Rocky Mountains rose majestically upward. The air was scented of pine, and I felt as though I had arrived in an enchanted land.

I returned a few days later for the Monday night community gathering. As I entered the meditation dome that evening, I sensed a very subtle yet tangible energy in the hall. This was the first of many encounters with the subtle at the ashram. The host remarked, almost in passing, of the force pervading the atmosphere in the dome. An interesting coincidence, I thought.

After the meditation program, we were asked to join Swami Shambhavananda in the adjacent house for questions and answers – a time when serious students as well as interested bystanders can learn about the ancient practice of Shambhava Yoga. I cannot say that as Swami entered the room I saw great lights and experienced the Divine, although many students have such first encounters. Instead, I saw a simple man with a charming presence. As I have come to realize, a deep connection with a spiritual practice need not manifest itself dramatically.

Swami addressed the crowd in a light and joking way. He had none of the pretenses of a holy man: he did not greet us with a holy gesture, nor did he give a long discourse on the merits of good action and the evils of sin. He began the evening by saying, "Hi, if anyone has any questions, please feel free to ask. If not, is dinner ready?"

I felt that there had to be more to a spiritual practice than contemplating the good and evil aspects of life and was pleased to see that yoga addressed topics which were beyond that realm. I was pleased to see that, during his discussion, Swami did not criticize other teachers and spiritual paths. Indeed, I have come to know that dogmatism is not in his character. Over the years, I have realized that Swami is a teacher who has transcended form and amassed content.

What I heard that evening was a precise, deep, and thorough understanding of the nature of the human condition and the path of Shambhava Yoga. The teachings were geared toward people who do not or cannot reject the material world in their spiritual pursuits. This practice teaches one how to use positive and negative emotions, anger and fear, basic drives, as well as the highest aspirations, to attain liberation. The stuff of human existence, it is shown, can be used for spiritual transformation.

It could be said, and accurately so, that the first page of Chapter One contains the necessary instruction to attain spiritual freedom. These are ancient and well-formed teachings expressed in a Western context. The simplicity of the instruction is not unique to the path of yoga. Christ's greatest teaching seems simple enough, "Love thy God with all thy heart and all thy might and all thy soul." Krishna teaches, "That yogi, whose mind remains unattached to external enjoyments, derives through meditation the unmixed joy which is inherent in the soul. That yogi, having completely identified with God, enjoys eternal bliss."

Although the essence of the teaching is simple, as we begin to tread the spiritual path, questions arise from the most mundane to the most profound. This book is an attempt to address the issues that a student faces from the beginning of the path to its ultimate conclusion. This progression is not linear: we may have a taste of the sublime while grappling with our stiff leg during meditation.

This book is a compilation of question and answer sessions which Swami holds at his ashrams in Eldorado Springs and Rollinsville, Colorado. Each chapter addresses important issues in a seeker's sadhana, or spiritual pursuit, and the excerpt of Swami's words at the beginning of each chapter summarizes its spirit.

The concept of divine energy, or Shakti, is interwoven with our philosophy and practice. This Shakti is none other than the pulsation of life that exists within you and within every other sentient being. At the culmination of the practice, one attains union, or yoga, with the Shakti and realizes that everything, whether seen or unseen, whether thought of or not, is a manifestation of the Kundalini Shakti. This is the goal of spiritual work.

– Ashok N. Srivastava, Ph.D.

Eldorado Canyon, near Boulder, Colorado

SPIRITUAL WORK

Avoiding the world does not bring about spiritual freedom. Spiritual freedom arises when you can surrender your tensions while maintaining an inner focus. Your attachments and desires will manifest when you are in that state. This gives you an opportunity to free yourself of illusion and go beyond your mind and emotions.

A test of attaining the spiritual heights is the ability to continually transcend yourself, your patterns, your attachments, and your emotions. Spiritual work is not a matter of accepting or rejecting the experiences of life. It is a matter of transcending these experiences and realizing your Inner Self. This is the true test of spiritual growth.

Real spiritual growth comes from the ability to transcend yourself over and over and over again. The internal crystallization most people feel secure with and try to fortify represents the tensions that limit their evolution. Spiritual growth arises when barriers are broken down. A seed planted in the soil surrenders itself completely and becomes a tree that bears flowers and fruit. The seed is totally lost in the soil and transforms into something else. In spiritual work, the lower, mundane self is shed so that the purity of the Inner Self can shine forth.

Often people try to have a spiritual life while hanging on to all their limitations and misconceptions. They do not dare venture beyond an area where they feel comfortable and can control and understand. Real growth comes to those who have a very deep and powerful wish to grow under all circumstances. They must be willing to go beyond their own limitations and tensions.

The secret of life that we are searching for is to be found inside. You do not need to voyage to the top of a mountain to find it. You will find it inside yourself, but you must have a burning wish in your heart to transcend your fear, limitations, and philosophy. In my spiritual work, I had major realizations at the death of a closely held ideal.

Meditation gives you the ability to turn your attention inside and experience a state beyond the mundane. It helps you go beyond the mind and emotions that define your world. Life brings plenty of opportunity to grow. One can either open up to the challenges of life and transcend them or build barriers and be crushed by them.

– Swami Shambhavananda
Eldorado Springs, Colorado
January 1994

Swami enjoying time with some of his students

Chapter One

Starting a Practice

You are not far from the state of pure Truth, pure consciousness, and pure bliss that you are seeking. Even when you are in your darkest hour, it is very close to you. All you have to do is untangle yourself from the external world. You will find that the states of despair and happiness are created by your mind. As long as you are bound by your mind you will suffer the consequences of its fluctuations. That is why beginning a spiritual practice will help you. Your problems will not magically disappear – you simply will not be distracted by them. You will develop a spiritual mechanism to deal with them.

How do I begin a spiritual practice?

Begin by disciplining the mind, the emotions, and the body with meditation. Sit comfortably and turn your attention inside. All of the obstacles and obscurations that have accumulated will arise in your mind. It is the consciousness with which you deal with these distractions that determines your spiritual evolution.

We are bound by these distractions. They obscure our view of the Truth. We don't need to reject them, but through right understanding, through clarity of mind, and through a transcendental state of consciousness, they begin to dissolve. That is how to gain liberation.

You are very close to the Divine. The perfection that you are seeking is as close as your breath. It is only because we get caught in a state of dualism that we feel separate from that experience.

What is the purpose of spiritual work?

The purpose of spiritual work is to experience a state of unconditional freedom, a state of love without attachment, a state of gratitude without reason. Try to experience joy without attachment to the object that you perceive as the source of your joy. This will give you a glimpse of your true nature. This is the experience of the Inner Self, of God, or of the Guru. These are just a few different names for the same experience.

Basically, people are looking for fulfillment, security, love, and happiness in places where it doesn't exist. Even though they feel they are doing good work and are being positive contributors, if they don't have an inner life, they will eventually feel that something in their life is missing.

When you are young, everything is beautiful, exciting, interesting, and new. You feel intoxicated with life. The next thing you know, you are a little older and are trying to obtain the same feeling from the experiences you had as a child. You wonder where it went. How come it is not as good as it used to be? As you become a little older, the body starts to give out. Your favorite foods don't taste the same, or you can't digest them once you eat them. You will find that your body is old, but you don't feel old.

People are often compelled by their ideas and desires for attaining certain symbols of happiness and success and fulfillment on an external level. They spend a tremendous amount of time and energy accumulating these symbols, only to find out that the material accumulation does not give them an inner sense of contentment.

Life can be fulfilling and rewarding. You can have a very positive experience, but it is determined by the level of inner consciousness you develop in yourself. Most people don't question their own existence. They are just in the accumulation mode where more is better. People with strong wills and strong minds will usually manifest things which then devour them.

If God or the Inner Self is within me, why can't I experience it?

Look for God with your heart, not with your eyes and not with your mind. Often people who are yearning for this experience are not searching with their heart enough. The experience of the Self is beyond thought and emotion and the mundane mind. As you practice, you will realize that this pure state of being is within you.

What is karma?

If you can understand the idea of karma, you will have a jump start on your spiritual practice. Karma literally means *action* in Sanskrit. The idea of karma is an extension of the law of cause and effect. All the decisions you have made in this life and past lives have given rise to your current situation. This means that your current situation is due to your past action.

Your life is a manifestation of your karma; it is not something imposed on you. Unconscious actions that arise from desire create karma, so it is hard not to create karma.

Through spiritual practice, one learns how to take experiences of life and consciously break them down into energy to further grow spiritually. After you experience an inner state of peace inside, you will be truly free if you can function from that awareness under all circumstances. That is the *real* work we do. The preliminary work is how to get past the stiff knees and sore backs and old rock songs. We are talking about spiritual enlightenment here, not an eight-week do-it-yourself course. It takes time and discipline.

A yogi is a person who develops the consciousness and awareness to use his or her life experience to evolve spiritually. The experience, in a sense, becomes fuel for spiritual development. If you live life with that attitude, every situation becomes an opportunity to grow, instead of everything being something to fear or reject or pursue.

Could you describe the process of spiritual growth?

It can be very tumultuous, very calm, very difficult, and also very simple. If everything were only nice and calm, you'd never grow. To grow spiritually, you need to be prepared to transcend all of your karma. That is all. You experience many cycles, and some seem more fun than others. Eventually you will realize that all experiences are just a manifestation of energy.

If you are experiencing a challenging situation, keep an inner focus. And if your life seems very pleasant, keep an inner focus nonetheless. A state of spiritual freedom isn't one where everything in the material world is the way you want it to be. Spiritual realization, spiritual maturity, spiritual energy, and spiritual power have nothing to do with having a perfect existence in the material world.

People are always trying to adjust their lives in the material world so that they can experience a sense of contentment and freedom. They say, "If only I had this kind of relationship, if only I had this much money, if only I had this degree, and this bill paid...." The list goes on and on. The adjustments are a temporary solution to a permanent problem. True freedom cannot be obtained through adjustments in the material world.

If I am not the mind, then who am I?

"If I am not the mind, then who am I?" This investigation has been going on in India for thousands of years. Keep asking yourself, "Who am I? Am I this finger? No, I am not really this finger. Am I this hand? Where does the I exist in this hand? Well, it is not really there. Where is it?" Try that investigation, and you will eventually find that you are the Inner Self, the witness of all action.

Don't you identify yourself with your mind?

No. The mind is simply an accumulation of experiences. That is not what I believe I am. When you meditate, you will realize that the thoughts are not what you really are. You begin to discover that there is a consciousness inside of you which is beyond the mind and is the essence of your true nature. The Self is not as complicated as the mind. This is my experience.

How do you know when you have separated the thoughts from your Self?

It is a very distinct experience. When it happens, you experience a state of being that is not affected by thoughts. The reason that we experience emotional ups and downs and pain and suffering and desire and attachment and revulsion is because we are identified with these thoughts. The reason there is no consistency or peace or ultimate satisfaction in life is because our mind is always fluctuating.

If something makes you feel good this week, next week it might make you feel bad. You like someone this week, and you hate the same person next week. These are just the fluctuations of the mind. The yogis say that since you are not the mind, there is no point in getting caught in it. It is better to turn your attention inside and discover your true nature, the state of being that exists behind these thoughts, behind all of these emotions and all of these experiences.

It is not a denial or a suppression of thoughts. You realize that they are just a nuisance. When you start to gain an awareness of the deeper levels of consciousness inside, it is easier to separate from thoughts. And then you are not feeding this process which is like a self-perpetuating machine: one thought leads to another which leads to 10,000 thoughts. One desire leads to 10,000 desires. It goes on and on and on.

When you discover the state inside that is separate from these fluctuations, you won't be so confused and tortured by your mind and all of the emotions that come and go. You will understand that you are not these. You are something totally pure.

The Self is defined as *Satchitananda*. *Sat* means Truth; *Chit* means pure consciousness and pure awareness; and *Ananda* means pure bliss. Pure bliss is a state of spiritual intoxication, a spiritual high that is the nature of your true Self.

Every experience you have in the material world that is pleasant in any way is just a pale reflection of this state which exists in you all the time. It does not come and go. Your awareness of it is what changes. If you are focused in the external world, then you feel separate and alone, or happy or unhappy. When you get more focused inside, you discover that these emotions are just states of mind. They are not what you really are.

What is the relationship of the body and consciousness?

The body is just the container. You must understand that every thought you have, every desire that wells up inside of you, every emotion you experience has created your body. Your actions from previous lives also give rise to your current state. In each lifetime, we incarnate into a circumstance and a body that allows us to fulfill our karma. You are not your body. To identify yourself with your body is similar to thinking that you are your car. You are not the car; you are the driver.

How can I know if my heart is speaking or my mind?

When the heart speaks, the mind is silent. The mind provides analysis and judgments, whereas the heart provides a sense of rightness. That is the difference. Many people say that they are following their heart. Usually they are following their desires.

When you can surrender the mind, when you can go beyond the mundane state of consciousness that judges and analyzes and get to a very deep state of awareness, you will have a very strong experience of your heart. You will be able to decide what will add to your spiritual growth and what will take away from it.

Ultimately, that should be the very question if you want to grow: what is going to help me evolve and what is going to distract me? You need to develop the ability to turn inside, quiet the mind, and access the higher consciousness that is within you. That Self has no motivation, no desire, and no agenda. The mind has plenty of agendas.

It's been my experience that when I'm in harmony with the Divine Energy, or *Kundalini Shakti*, as it is called in Sanskrit, when I'm not coming from a place of attachment and desire, I don't really encounter many obstacles. Of course, there have been problems, but I have found that when I am working from my heart, the world seems magical.

This power that exists within you can remove major obstacles very easily. I flowed through situations that I thought could be very troublesome. There were other times that I felt absolutely right, and I got smashed. That's how I developed the ability to discriminate between my mind and my heart. If you never take a chance, you will never grow.

Meditation

What is meditation?

It is just another name for not thinking. It is not a matter of trying not to think; rather, it is a matter of separating yourself from your thoughts. There is a big difference. Trying not to think is a hopeless battle. Letting go of the thoughts, in a sense witnessing them and turning your attention inside, will give you an awareness of a different perspective, a different sense of self.

Most of our identity is tied up in the words, thoughts, and pictures in our mind. We usually assume that our thoughts define ourselves. Actually, our thoughts create the world we experience. The mind is infinite in its capacity to create multiplicity – one thought leads to two thoughts, which lead to 10,000 thoughts. There are many methods to discipline the mind – some are more direct than others. Meditation will help you understand the nature of the mind and will lead you to the experience of your true nature. Meditation is a method to experience a state of consciousness beyond thought and mundane perception.

In the *Yoga Sutras of Patanjali*, a classical text on yoga, the mind is likened to an ocean with endless waves. Meditation is a process of stilling these thought waves in the mind. People think that stopping all thoughts is bad because they believe it could make the mind dull or hypnotized. Actually, a clear and quiet mind is a very powerful tool. A weak mind can't stay still, needs constant stimulation, and is always engaged in plotting and scheming and planning. People with this type of mind never find peace. They pursue more and more stimulation. They read more, they watch more, they consume more. Finally, they burn out.

How does one meditate?

The technique of meditation that we use is the *Ham Sah* practice, which is very simple and extremely profound. It is a method to recognize the pure state of consciousness that already exists within you. You are not looking for something you do not already have.

The *Ham Sah* practice can give you a very profound and extraordinary experience, yet it is very simple. Sit quietly and comfortably, and take a few moments to relax your body and mind. Notice your breath as you inhale and exhale. Don't try to alter or modify your breath, just observe it. As you relax during the inhalation, you will begin to hear the sound of *Ham* as the breath enters your body. Then, as you exhale, you will hear the sound of *Sah*. This is the sound of the exhalation. The *Ham Sah* mantra, or phrase, is continually present, whether you are aware of it or not. The process of meditation is to become consciously aware of this breath flow.

The inhalation and exhalation are similar to a swinging pendulum. As a pendulum swings back and forth, there is a moment when all motion stops, and the pendulum changes directions. Similarly, with the breath, between the inhalation and exhalation, the breath stops and changes directions. If you focus on the point of stillness between the *Ham* and the *Sah*, you will find that not only does the breath stop, but the mind stops as well. The breath and the mind are intertwined in this way.

This moment of silence, this moment where all mental, emotional, and physical activity ceases, is the gateway to the Inner Self. It is the experience of the pure consciousness that exists within you. As you sit in meditation, you might also notice that in between one thought and another thought there is the same instant, the same moment where all activity stops. Focus your awareness on these still points between thoughts and between breaths. When you begin the practice, you might notice that your mind engages in some kind of activity: thinking about yesterday, or tomorrow's agenda, or some other distraction. When this happens, simply bring your attention back to the practice and don't worry about the distractions.

When the mind becomes less agitated you begin to experience pure consciousness, or the witness state. You begin to identify with the witness of all experience and activity. This witness is perfectly quiet, perfectly content, and dwells in perfect Truth and bliss. This is an experience of your true nature.

I have a question regarding the use of Ham Sah technique during meditation. Sometimes when I take in the breath I find I have to stretch the Ham to make it last the entire inhalation.

Don't worry about making the mantra last through the whole inhalation. You are focusing on the technique too much instead of the spirit of the technique. Just witness the natural rhythm of your breath. When you start applying too much technique, you are using your will and your mind too much. What you should do is listen to the inhalation and exhalation. Your listening should be very alert and very clear and not contrived and not forced. It should be natural.

And when your mind starts to wander, just listen to the sound of your breath and the sound of the mantra in your breath. In that way, bring all your attention back inside. It's that simple. It's the way to develop an awareness of the inner realm.

Can you only have one breath with the Ham Sah mantra or can you have two, or is that too contrived?

Again, you are too focused on the technique. The *Ham Sah* practice is simply observing your inhalation and exhalation. Don't think about how you breathe in and out – just breathe in and out. You are not trying to be a bellows! You are just trying to observe a natural breath flow. This is a good exercise for learning how to let go of your inner tensions and relax.

The more you get caught up in the technique, the more barriers you create. This is a method to experience a state which already exists inside of you. You will recognize this fact through commitment and practice.

How much time should I spend meditating?

You should get up in the morning and take a shower and meditate for a half hour to 45 minutes before breakfast. Before dinner, meditate again. After you gain some experience, you will carry the meditative state through your daily activities. You won't need a special place to meditate. Your whole day will become a meditation.

How can I know whether my meditation is productive or whether I am just in a stupor?

Sitting in a stupor leads to a very dull state, whereas a productive meditation brings about clarity of mind. Have you ever experienced a state where your mind was empty and totally clear and thoughts weren't coming and going? That is a good meditative state. You can be in that state of clarity in the midst of total chaos in the external world. The clarity doesn't come and go. It is your awareness of it that wanes.

When I meditate, I can quiet my mind and experience a state without thoughts. I feel like I've missed the point of meditating, because I've never gone beyond that.

No, you haven't missed the point. Just sit in that quiet state. The problem arises when you feel that you have to *do* something. That feeling gives rise to doership, which gives rise to anxiety, pressure, and tension. What you have to do is sink into a very deep state of meditation. In that stillness, in that quiet space in between thoughts, exists the gateway to your enlightenment. But the minute doership gets involved, you pull yourself away from that state. Certainly in that quiet state you still feel the body, the breath, and the space around you. But as you surrender your attachments, you will become aware of the deeper levels of consciousness that exist within you. This experience gives you a glimpse of your true nature, which is beyond the mind and its fluctuations. It is only the superficial mind that wants to yank you out of that quiet state.

In our culture, the mind is worshipped, but that's kind of like worshipping a pair of pliers. If used correctly, the mind is a good tool for success in the material world, but it cannot provide the solution to the basic questions we have as human beings. By learning to discipline the mind, it is possible to get in touch with a deeper level of consciousness, a deeper sense of Self. It is there that the answers can be found. People are afraid of losing something by quieting their mind. What they lose is duality, pain, suffering, confusion, and all the things that drive them nuts.

The meditations I usually experience seem like little steps toward the Self. Yet tonight, I felt as though I was going to take a huge leap. It scared me, and I was dismayed that I was frightened.

It is wonderful that you felt close to your Inner Self. We are all much closer to the state of pure awareness than we imagine. It feels as though we are far away from it, but we aren't. The reason that you felt frightened is because of your attachments and desires. When you start to psychically separate from that false identity, it can be a little unsettling.

I understand the value of meditation but I gain a great deal from reading spiritual books. Could you address the relationship between having an intellectual understanding and meditation?

Having an intellectual understanding of yoga is certainly important. Often people don't have much understanding about their mind, about the nature of the mind and the nature of *Samsaric*, or material existence. But in my opinion, there is absolutely no replacement for meditation.

After I started my practice, I came to a stage where the scriptures and ancient Yogic philosophies that I read made sense to me. The readings made sense because they were based upon my own inner experience. The readings clarified that experience.

I recently read the Bhagavad Gita and experienced an understanding that I wouldn't have had 10 years ago.

If you are truly growing and evolving and you read a great spiritual book such as the *Bhagavad Gita*, it will have a profound effect on you. You will realize a level of Truth you haven't seen before. But the depth of your understanding won't be the same if you just study it without an inner experience.

Many people who read sacred texts don't have a full understanding because they have never had the experience themselves. They are trying to experience the meaning solely through the intellect. The intellect is faulty in that realm. The Truth is something that exists beyond words. This idea is in virtually every spiritual tradition. There are thousands of pages of spiritual texts, but they cannot encompass the Truth. There is knowledge, wisdom, and experience which cannot be contained in books.

Mantra

What is mantra?

A mantra is a set of words that is repeated silently or while chanting. When repeated silently, the practice of mantra is called japa. The mantra *OM NAMAH SHIVAYA* is a powerful psychic purification tool – it can clean out all the accumulated emotional baggage that you carry around. It will enable you to arrive in a meditative state.

It is good to have an understanding of the meaning of the mantra. When you are repeating *OM NAMAH SHIVAYA*, you are recognizing and acknowledging the divinity that exists within you. *Shiva* is a name for the pure consciousness that exists within you.

OM NAMAH SHIVAYA also has a powerful sound vibration. If you give yourself to the mantra, whether you are chanting or repeating it quietly, you will find that the sound vibration is in tune with the conscious energy or Inner Self. Mantra is a very powerful spiritual tool – it will take you to an experience of your higher consciousness.

There are many kinds of mantras in our world. This mantra was given to me by my teacher, Swami Muktananda, and is one that he used for his own practice and his spiritual attainment. So it is a living mantra. It has tremendous power and the ability to give you a very deep level of inner experience. The more you use it, the more you work with it, the stronger the vibration becomes in you. You do not have to believe in it or accept it. All you need to do is use it.

Many people don't realize that the way you receive a mantra affects your experience of it. If you receive the mantra from someone who has used it for their own attainment, it has a different effect than if the same mantra were obtained in some other way. Someone could give you the same mantra, but you will have a much different experience than if you received it directly from Baba Muktananda. This has to do with consciousness: the consciousness that gave you the mantra and the consciousness that received the mantra. It makes a big difference.

What is the experience of the mantra OM NAMAH SHIVAYA?

You can simply repeat the words *OM NAMAH SHIVAYA* and have one level of experience. But there are many levels of experience in dealing with mantra. It's much better than repeating other kinds of phrases like "Oh, I feel so depressed," which is what many people repeat in their mind. Repeating *OM NAMAH SHIVAYA* has a deep effect on the energy centers in the subtle body. It has a vibratory effect on the subtle energy channels and causes a purification. If you practice mantra with clarity and with real openness, you will start to experience pure consciousness.

It is important to understand that the power of a practice comes from the dedication you have to it. People are always looking for an outside force to give them a spiritual experience. But it's the feeling you cultivate and the discipline you bring to your own practice that will determine your experience.

What is the best way to do mantra repetition?

Often! When you are meditating, it is best to do japa, or mantra repetition, in conjunction with the breath. When you are driving, walking, doing dishes, or cooking, just repeat the mantra silently. It purifies the mind and focuses it. A weak mind can't accomplish much.

Why do we chant the mantra?

Chanting bathes your psychic system. It's a good practice to attune yourself to the subtle vibration. While you are chanting, it's important to keep your attention fixed on the chant and not allow your mind to wander. It takes consciousness, understanding, application, and practice. It can give you a very profound experience.

I had tremendous resistance to chanting and mantra practice when I met Baba Muktananda, since at the time, I used to only meditate. Then I walked into a chant that lasted three days without stop. It had such a profound effect on me. I could feel there was a real power and quality in the practice. So I made an effort to assimilate that. So it is the mantra, and the feeling that you have for the mantra, and the connection to the Lineage that makes it alive and powerful. Mantra repetition amplifies the Shakti, which pulsates within everyone.

I can't seem to stop crying during chanting.

That is good. As your psychic system is cleansed, you may feel emotion well up inside. This is a release of tension and emotion that has blocked your psychic system. As you give yourself more to the chant, a purification will take place. It will really flush out negativity and tension. Your energy centers are responding to the Shakti that is behind the chant. Try to relax to facilitate your desire to release tension, instead of dwelling on the emotion.

Does it take a long time to release this tension?

When I went to see Baba Muktananda for the first time, I think I cried for four days! It didn't matter if I was chanting or not. I just cried. I was profoundly affected by his energy. Maybe you are being profoundly affected by his energy too. Just open up to it and don't suppress it. Allow the process to complete itself.

All our experiences are stored in our psychic system in the same way that residues build up in a plumbing system. Our memories go deeper than many people believe. When you come into an environment with a lot of energy, such as this ashram, and you get a little spiritual nourishment, you can let go of many of the experiences that are stored in your subtle body. It is not really a psychological process. It is a cleansing of the psyche. Many people come here and feel something deep. Some get angry, some people feel sad, and some cry for joy. When I met Baba, I wasn't crying because I felt bad. I was just so happy. I was in an ecstatic state. In the practice of Shambhava Yoga, these are symptoms of an inner awakening.

Maintaining an Inner Focus

I have really enjoyed my meditation experience at this ashram. How can I maintain my experience when I return home?

Just do the practice; that is all. The connection to our practice and our lineage of teachers has been made. If you pay attention to it and relate to it, the connection will deepen.

It is very hard for me to develop and maintain a spiritual life at home.

It is possible. Ultimately, it is not whether you are at the ashram or not, it is the depth of your experience that determines your evolution. When I started my spiritual practice, I would only see my teacher, Rudi, every few months.

I was living in his ashram, but he wasn't there all the time. So I learned how to develop my spiritual work without his physical presence.

I was very focused on spiritual work, but I became very discontent because my goal seemed so far off. How do you deal with that discontent? Now I am almost a skeptic!

These are the wild swings of the mind. The antidote for that condition is to establish a regular practice. The mind is much like a horse that has never had a saddle on it. It needs to be disciplined. If you create a structured, disciplined practice and work at it every day, whether you feel at one with the universe or tiny and insignificant, you will obtain results. You will develop the ability to ride the waves of the mind, so to speak. Being ecstatic one day and a skeptic the next are just fluctuations in your mind. Meditation will begin to smooth all that out for you. The fluctuations you are experiencing are not unusual.

When I first started, I was very enthusiastic myself. After I met my first teacher, Swami Rudrananda, and saw the level of consciousness that is possible, I was amazed and a little bit horrified, too. I looked at my own inner condition and was horrified at the amount of psychic garbage that I was carrying. But I just started practicing.

You are not far from the state of consciousness you are seeking. Even when you are in your darkest hour, it is very close to you. All you have to do is untangle yourself from the external world. As long as you are bound by your mind, you will suffer the consequences of its fluctuations. That is why beginning a practice will help you. Your problems will not magically disappear; they simply won't distract you. You will develop a spiritual mechanism to deal with them.

I have done my spiritual practice for quite a while, but I realize that there is no strong reason why I do it. I don't know what is driving me.

The most important reason to pursue spiritual practice is to have a realization. That is the ultimate goal. A by-product of that pursuit is that your experience of life will change tremendously. It's not so much that the outer manifestations will change, but your experience of the manifestations will change as your consciousness evolves. As you expand, the experience of your life changes dramatically. Your life becomes easier because you become more skillful in dealing with it. This is a by-product of meditation.

I don't really do my practice because I have a deep wish to grow. Instead, I do it because I feel I should. Do you have any advice?

That's no problem. Often when one starts a practice it is out of a sense of duty. If the practice is real, you'll reach a point where you can see into your own condition. Then you'll have a great desire to practice. My teacher once said that if you really want some insight into yourself, lock yourself inside a room for a day and keep repeating, "I want to grow, I want to grow...." Listen to the shallowness, the lack of commitment and sincerity, and the resistance that begins to overwhelm you. Seeing your inner condition is very stimulating for inner growth.

I want to know how to accelerate my spiritual growth.

The way to accelerate spiritual growth is to let go of your tensions and relax. Once you have realized the impermanence of this world, and the transitory nature of pleasure and pain, you just need to quiet your mind and open your heart. You need to surrender all the desire that you have, even for growth. Keep surrendering all of the mind stuff. The more you let go, the more that will bubble up. You will surrender your spiritual fantasies. What is left after deeply surrendering these thoughts and emotions is the state of pure consciousness that the scriptures speak of. It is really important that you find a spiritual practice that works for you and do it.

Spiritual growth is much like a tree. Just settle down, let your roots sink in, create a simple, disciplined life, keep your heart open, and you will evolve. Everything you need to let go of to experience your true nature will manifest. When you become really serious about it, you don't have to go anywhere or do anything. You just have to sit down and open up your heart.

Yoga and Religion

What is God?

People have many definitions of God. Many Westerners have a concept of God that is dualistic in nature: a God that continually judges us and watches our every move. This is a dualistic view, since it draws a distinction between us and God.

In the Yogic tradition, God is seen as pure consciousness. It is not seen as something separate from us at all. This spark of divinity, this pure, all-pervading consciousness, exists in every sentient being. The reason we do not experience this state of consciousness is because we exist in a bound and contracted state. Through meditation and stilling the fluctuations of the mind, we can discover that Divinity within us. We can experience a state of nondualism, a state of unity.

Pure consciousness is not something that is easily encompassed by the mind because the mind exists in a contracted, dualistic state. It has a sense of separateness and a sense of ego. The process of spiritual growth has to do with the dissolution of this contracted state.

Is meditation a religion?

People used to ask Baba Muktananda this question. Baba would say that meditation is a religion in the same way that sleep is a religion. If you can call sleep a religion, you can call meditation a religion.

Meditation is a conscious process. You are accessing a deeper level of consciousness, which is the source of your energy. The Inner Self isn't the property of any religion. No one owns it. Everyone calls it by a different name. The experience of the Inner Self is pure consciousness and is beyond religion. Try to have your own experience of it.

How does yoga interact with the Western religions?

I think that people who study meditation and yoga see the Truth in all traditions. Unfortunately, it generally doesn't come the other direction.

That's what I'm finding. yoga seems to describe some very basic principles.

Yoga has been around for more than 5,000 years, and the Truth hasn't changed in that time. Our perceptions of the Truth have changed. yoga is based on an ancient philosophy that does not separate humans and God. The tradition teaches that the divine consciousness which has created the seen and unseen universe exists within every sentient being. It doesn't matter whether we judge someone to be good or bad, because that spark of divinity is within everyone.

Meditation allows you to discover your inner divinity and helps you let go of your ego and your limitations. Then you can merge with the divine consciousness spontaneously. In a sense, you have a spontaneous recognition of your own Self.

Could you say something about mixing different spiritual practices?

Well, it's a little like going into a chemistry class mixing different chemicals. Sometimes you get an explosion, sometimes you make a chemical reaction that smells very bad. The outcome is unpredictable.

It's important to choose a path and stick with it until it bears fruit. Many people in our culture jump from practice to practice. It's like searching for water by digging a well two feet deep, finding nothing, moving to another site and digging another two feet, again finding nothing, and going somewhere else and digging five feet, and still finding nothing. You'll never find water unless you pick a site and dig deeply. It's important to pick a practice and commit to it. Otherwise, when you meet resistance, you'll switch to a different one. It is my belief that if you find another path that serves you spiritually, it is not necessary to follow the practice that I teach.

The meditation practice that you teach seems to be very similar in some ways to Buddhist traditions.

The meditative practice that I teach and have been doing for a long time has its counterpart in Buddhism– both the Indian and the Tibetan traditions and the Eastern Zen schools. The practice of yoga predates all of these Buddhist traditions. Each tradition has encompassed some aspect of the yogic practices.

My Guru, Swami Rudrananda, was very close to Eido Roshi and other Zen teachers. I am also very close to many Tibetan Lamas. We are all basically Yogis. I've spent time in Japanese Zen monasteries, and in Korean and Tibetan monasteries. The practice that I do is very compatible with what they are doing. I guess we could have sat down and debated about the semantics of what we believed, but we didn't.

Padmasambhava, "the Lotus-born," is the master Yogi who brought Buddhism to Tibet

Swami with Tibetan friends at Shoshoni's Buddha Rocks

Swami Shambhavananda (Swamiji)

Chapter Two

SURRENDER

In a spiritual context, "surrender" is the ability to separate from the fluctuations of your mind and turn your attention inside. In this way, instead of accepting or rejecting the mind, you simply observe it. You will begin to understand that you are something much more expansive than thoughts. People identify themselves with their thoughts and emotions. Certainly you have a body and thoughts and emotions. But the purpose of meditation is discovering your true nature, a state of being that is beyond those.

What is surrender?

Surrender is the ability to let go of your patterns, emotions, and tensions. The way to surrender spiritually is to let go of the mind – don't suppress it and don't engage it either. Simply observe it as though it were a movie. Surrender does not mean that you give your will or mind to a person or a group. Real spiritual growth has to do with the ability to consciously open up to all the blocks and tensions in yourself and to deeply let go.

It is as though you are holding onto a big anchor at the bottom of the ocean. All you need to do is let go, and you will rise to the top. But we like our anchor, and we are very attached to it. We have put time and energy into creating our persona, identity, and limitations, which are the building blocks of our anchor. Our life has become a process of building and hanging on to this anchor. Spiritual growth has to do with the total annihilation of that process. On the one hand, it seems silly that we would not let go of that anchor; but on the other hand, to let go of it is the most terrifying thing in the world.

That is the nature of surrender. It has to do with opening up to your limitations and simply releasing them. Your greatest limitation is your definition of life and your experiences. Try to see through the illusions you have created. They are very powerful and we cling to them desperately. But once you deeply let go and get in touch with the inner consciousness, it is like taking a deep breath after being suffocated for a long time. You will feel relieved and more expansive.

Meditation is the ultimate remedy, because it works at the source of the problem, instead of at the symptom. You are looking for solutions to the lack of fulfillment and nourishment in your life in a direction where they do not exist. We intuitively know that, because we try to solve our internal problems over and over again, but they do not get solved. I am not giving you anything you do not already have. I am just making you aware of what is already there.

How can I know if I am surrendering properly or not?

If you have managed to surrender a deep tension, you will feel a lightness inside. The space that was holding that tension will expand. For instance, if you feel a deep sorrow which becomes all encompassing, you are indulging in the emotion and not surrendering it. On the other hand, if you feel a deep emotion start to rise in you, simply focus your attention inside, breathe into the heaviness that you feel, and let it go. That is real surrender.

On an energetic level, the energy center in your subtle body where this particular tension is stored will be cleansed, and a feeling of lightness will spread through you. You might not be able to analyze it, but there will be a tangible difference in your being. When this surrender occurs, many people don't feel comfortable. They doubt their experience. As they analyze it, the lightness gets dimmer and dimmer. Soon, they feel lousy again.

Surrender doesn't make you a victim or somebody's doormat. Surrender makes you stronger because it frees you of all the attachments that bind you. People dream about spirituality and the miraculous. They would like to have that experience, but the reason it never comes is that they never ask deep enough. They never really focus their attention inside. It's like trying to see the sun with your head in the sand.

When I surrender some attachments, they seem to get stronger. Am I feeding the tension rather than surrendering it?

No. You may not realize the depth of the attachment. Some things that you identify as problems or negative patterns in yourself have a much deeper root system than you realize. They are like yucca plants. You may whack off the top, but the darned thing pops up again!

In our culture, people think that manipulating things in their mind will have some long-lasting effect. But the change only takes place in the mind, and then the mind changes again and again and again. The only solution is to transcend the mind.

We go through life making temporary adjustments to ourselves. Most are satisfied with the temporary solutions. But through meditation and a deep inner wish to grow, you can realize the permanent solution. That's what having a spiritual life is all about. It's not what you wear, or what you eat, or where you live. A spiritual life is one where you work toward surrendering the limited view of yourself.

I want to learn how to release to God. My life has so many troubles that I am at a loss as to what to do.

The more you focus on the Inner Self, the easier it will become. It may seem scary. It's hard to let go of that fear. But that is what your practice is all about. It is to teach you that inside of you is something far greater than fear and tension. By meditating and opening up and accessing a deep level of consciousness, you will obtain the solution to your problems. But if you stay focused outside, in a sense, it feeds them.

Have you heard the story of the boy who found the wish-fulfilling gem? A boy was wandering through a jungle in India and found a wish-fulfilling gem. He didn't know what it was. And he thought, "Boy, I sure am hungry!" A beautiful table full of food and refreshments manifested, and he was satisfied. And he thought, "Wow, where did this come from? This is really great! I'm so full. It would really be nice to find a place to take a nap." So a big house manifested. Every thought that he had became reality. Then he thought, "This must be some kind of enchanted forest. There is probably a demon around here somewhere." A big demon manifested. The boy thought, "He's probably going to eat me up." And the demon ate him up!

That is what our mind does to us. We feed our tendencies and patterns instead of recognizing the Self. To feed fears and anxieties is just giving them life. So when that starts to happen just internalize, follow your breath, and start to do your practice. When you turn inside and dig deep in your spiritual practice, you create the potential for the problems to be resolved.

Anger and Sadness

My life seems to go through cycles of happiness and sadness.

This is the dilemma of human existence. When we find something that is pleasant, we do it. And soon because of our tensions and our desires, we turn heaven into hell. The practice of Shambhava Yoga is to work through the "heaven" and "hell" to find that the Self is in both.

You can't reason yourself into a state of enlightenment, but a certain amount of understanding is necessary. You have to discipline your body, mind, and emotions. Then it will be easier to experience the perfection that is already there. People get caught in emotions or desire and try to accept or reject them. This week they feel really bad. Next week they feel really blissful. Next week they find true love! Three weeks later they lose true love. A month later they find God, and a month later they lose God. It just goes on!

So engage in the battles of your material life, and pursue your Self with sincerity and integrity. Once you have an experience of the Inner Self, you will want a deeper experience. Eventually, all distractions will fall away.

Could you talk more about surrender and sadness?

Surrender is the ability to let the sadness go without getting your mind tangled up in it. Sadness is stored in the psychic system. As you start to evolve, and the Kundalini energy moves through the energy centers, very deep and powerful emotions will surface. If you relate to them in some way, or get involved with them, it just compounds the problem. What you have to do is surrender the emotion. Simply let it go. Only after you have transcended the emotion does some kind of realization come. You might find that there was no identifiable reason for your sadness. The realization will show you how that particular emotion has affected so many elements of your life. You will see that this little psychic knot was coloring your experience of the whole world. Having that realization isn't an intellectual process. It is a process of inner spiritual work. You will even need to surrender the realization, because yesterday's realization becomes tomorrow's obstacle.

What is the difference between surrendering an emotion or just going with it?

You do not want to go with it; you want to watch it leave. There is a big difference. Use the practice to open up to where the sadness is in your psychic system. Breathe into that space, and the sadness will dissolve. Keep going deeper into the practice. You might feel that you need to go deeper than ever before, but you can remove the root of the sadness if you keep working.

Many people feel that deep emotions should be expressed.

This was a popular concept in the '60s and early '70s. People would indulge in emotions such as screaming or yelling. The more you indulge those activities, the deeper the pattern you create in your psychic system. So, every time you repeat an action, it increases your burden. But if you can transmute the emotion, you will find that it is just energy under pressure. Break it down into a flow of energy and you will feel yourself becoming free. yoga does not suppress or deny deep emotions. Instead of expressing them, they can be dissolved.

How can I eliminate the surface noise of emotions and thoughts during meditation?

The way you eliminate thoughts and emotions is to surrender them. If you do not feed them, they will not grow. But if you wrestle with them, they will consume an enormous amount of energy to no avail.

How do you work with a situation that brings up anger?

Anger will do more damage to your own psyche than it will to anybody else. Even if you can overcome someone with your anger, it does more damage to you than you could do to them. Unless you have that understanding, you are just hurting yourself.

So what you have to do is open your heart beyond that emotion. In the psychic system, anger is just a contracted energy. It ties you in a knot. As soon as you become aware of that process, you have to reverse it. But you don't reverse it with your mind. Anger is like a fire burning out of control. By using the breath to open your psychic system, you'll take the fuel right out of the fire. The best time to do it is when you feel really angry.

In the beginning, when you are unconscious and unfocused, you don't have the luxury of ignoring anger. You have to take care of it. Many situations demand that you have to respond whether it is from anger or calmness.

As you get more skillful and more disciplined in your practice, your ability to deal with adversity will increase. That is the growth process. People say, "First I am going to become perfect and then I will take care of my responsibilities." It doesn't work that way. You respond from the context that you are in now. You have to try to deal with difficulties by using the practice. That is what makes the practice and the inner discipline real and creates the foundation inside of you. You actually use the practice to build the foundation within the chaotic situations of your life. It is within the tension and the drama of life that there is an opportunity for real understanding, for real growth.

Even if I work the way you have described, I still feel anger and negativity toward people, and I don't know how to deal with it.

It is most important to deal with your reaction to your own negativity, anger, and judgmental attitude. When doing spiritual work, don't concern yourself with the apparent reason for your anger. Learn how to work with it in yourself. The way you do that is, when you feel anger arise in yourself, surrender the emotion. Often we carry around so much negativity. We think that we see the imperfection in everyone else, but what we are really seeing is our own imperfection.

Patterns of Emotion

From where do our patterns of behavior arise?

According to the Yogic tradition, the actions we have performed in our past leave impressions that exist in the subtle body. These impressions cause you to desire and pursue more action. These tendencies are with us from past life times, not just the events of the last week. When you impulsively respond to an urge, you create karma. Each time you do that, you are creating one more bit of karma. When you truly realize this fact, you become very careful about how you live.

If you spend time purifying your mind and disciplining your body, you can tilt the scales. The whole point of yoga and meditation is to improve your internal condition. In a sense, your karma is burned up in the fire of yoga.

How can I change my old patterns?

To change old patterns in the way that you are thinking is virtually impossible. To say, "I see this old pattern, and I want to change it. I'm going to be this way because that way is bad and this way is good" – that is psychology. The yogic perspective is quite different.

In yoga, you don't focus on patterns, whether you view them to be positive or negative. In a sense, you are feeding them by focusing on them. You don't create a fantasy about some other way that you would like to be. Instead, you turn deeply into your own Inner Self and discover the perfection that is already there.

When you experience the vastness of the inner consciousness, the outer patterns don't have a hold on you. So patterns can be totally dissolved by deepening your spiritual practice. And you don't have to do anything. Baba Muktananda called it the natural state.

When I see my inner condition, I feel discouraged. What advice do you have for me?

That often happens when people first start the practice, because they do not have an awareness of their Self. All they see is their own emotional baggage, and they get a little freaked out and try not to deal with it. So they just slam the door on their problems and pretend they don't exist.

A spiritual practice helps free you of your emotional baggage. When you have a toothache, you have to go to the doctor. You might not want the tooth to be removed, but it will just get worse. People think that because they can slam the door on their internal condition their problems will disappear. They won't – the problems will just get worse.

My life seems too difficult for me to handle. I am not sure what to do.

You have to rise above your mundane understanding and level of basic resistance on a physical level. It doesn't take much to function on a physical level.

Some people's lives are a little overwhelming for them because they are inefficient and unconscious about how they use their energy. They haven't understood how to efficiently function in the physical realm. They are dragged around by their mind and emotions. They are basically living a very unconscious life. As you develop in your spiritual discipline and capacity, you become very conscious of how you use your energy, and you become very efficient. Even if you have difficulties, it doesn't take much energy to deal with them. I explain this idea to people in terms they relate to and understand: money.

If you have a very large income of let's say one million dollars a year, then obstacles that are a real problem to poor people aren't so much of a problem for you. If you total your car, it's no big deal to go get another one.

On the other hand, if you are unemployed and don't have much money, everything seems to be an obstacle. So life becomes an enormous struggle. Many people are expending an enormous amount of energy just to sustain a material existence.

Personal energy works the same way. If you lead a conscious life and use your energy efficiently, the problems of day-to-day existence are not too difficult to handle. By "efficiently using your energy," I mean that you bring yourself to the point where your energy is not being drained by your own desires and emotions, which are like holes in your bucket of energy. You can then use your energy for spiritual pursuits.

Swami Shambhavananda offering prasad (special sweets)

Chapter Three

The Teacher

Quiet your mind and be as deeply open as you can be. Then you might get an answer without asking a question.

What is the function of the teacher on the spiritual path?

The teacher is someone with whom you feel a connection and who has the capacity to initiate you and help you along the path. At first the teacher may seem like a parent. If the relationship evolves, he or she may become like a brother or sister. Eventually, you may become friends. My personal conviction is that I would not have had the grace in my life or the experience that I've had in meditation and my spiritual practice without the direct help and intervention of my Gurus.

It is not the teacher's job to control the student's life. The teacher's job is to teach. If a student is genuinely sincere about the relationship, then he or she will really hear what is being said. Most people hear about 30% of what is said, and the rest just bounces off.

What is a Guru?

The Guru is another name for the Inner Self, which is the higher consciousness that exists in everyone. A physical Guru is someone who has attained that realization and exists in that state.

Can one get guidance from reading spiritual books?

If you have to relate to a living, breathing individual, it makes your spiritual experience more real. It is in a personal relationship with a teacher that all of the difficulties in the practice can be explored and overcome. You can have a vision of a great being during meditation and receive initiation, but it is necessary to have a living teacher with whom you can work.

Spiritual books are as important for one's spiritual development as science books are for medical students. But, as in medicine, reading is not sufficient. You never hear of a medical student doing brain surgery just by reading a book. Similarly, you don't attain the spiritual heights simply by reading. You have to go through the schooling.

The teacher inspires and challenges you, and helps you evolve and grow. That is the whole purpose of a teacher. The teacher is someone who has walked the path and is a little ahead of you, so he or she knows it well. The teacher can give you support, encouragement, inspiration, and some energy to evolve. But the teacher cannot do the work for you. It is sad to see people who have studied so much philosophy and spirituality maintain a distance between themselves and their spiritual pursuits.

The Student

Is there a specific way that the teacher-student relationship is supposed to look externally?

No. Each person has a different relationship with the teacher. Really, the student sets the tone of the relationship. When you find a teacher for whom you have respect and love, and you wish to receive some kind of teaching, the way the relationship evolves has to do with your own tension.

When I went to see Baba Muktananda, he was known as a tough Guru. In the '60s and '70s, he was known for being very demanding. That's because he had a lot to give. Because of that, I was expecting a certain amount of difficulty. But I didn't get a drop of it, because I surrendered my inner tensions. I was treated like a long-lost grandson and a prince. I was treated extremely benevolently, with love and grace. It was amazing.

Do you know immediately when you have met your teacher?

No. When I met Rudi, he scared me to death. I wanted to get as far away from him as possible. I knew what he said was the Truth, but I just didn't want to accept it. My immediate reaction wasn't deep love and devotion. It was more like terror.

I remember when I first met him. I was at the back of an audience of 700 people. I could barely see him on the stage. He began to talk and looked right at me, and I began to slump in my chair to try to hide behind the people in front of me. That was my experience. Rudi was not good for my ego at all!

If you really want to grow, you have to be willing to walk through the fire that burns your ego and destroys your limitations. Sometimes that's not pleasant, so the bond to the teacher has to be strong. If you look at the lives and experiences of teachers such as Muktananda or Ramakrishna, you'll find that their lives were not always steeped in bliss.

I always measure teachers by the experience that they can offer. I have met very highly evolved beings, and also many who were lacking in understanding and depth.

Could you talk about being a student?

When people come to me as a teacher, I generally leave them alone and see whether they are serious about doing the practice. Because really, it's up to the student. I can sit here and profess all kinds of philosophy, but until you do a basic practice, I cannot be of much real help. When you are a serious student, you attract a worthy teacher. That has been my experience.

If a person really wants to study, it's like getting a Ph.D.: it takes time and commitment. People with spiritual discipline will certainly progress.

If you want to know what I know and experience what I experience, all you have to do is open up and surrender your attachments. Nothing is withheld from anyone – it's that simple! If you can let go of your mind and your emotions and deeply open your heart and resonate in the same place that I'm resonating from, you'll experience what I experience.

You mentioned "resonating with the teacher." What does that mean?

It means that you don't relate from your mind, but rather from your heart. That is all. If you are connecting on a purely intellectual level, you'll only get a small portion of the knowledge that is available.

But if you can open your heart, you will connect with the energy, or Shakti, that is available. Ultimately, the Truth can't be expressed in words. It is not transmitted through words. It is transmitted through your own inner experience. So you have to open up to that. So we Swamis yak, yak, yak, and occupy your mind until you finally open your heart and feel something.

What are the qualities of a good student?

I think you should have a very deep commitment to spiritual growth, to reaching your spiritual enlightenment and full spiritual potential. That is very important. To work consistently with deep commitment over a long period of time will really bring growth. You have to realize that you are working for your own growth, and only you can do your spiritual practice.

Should students fully turn their will over to their teacher?

Most people have fully turned their will over to Madison Avenue, so they can't give their will to anyone else. They are motivated by all their desires, which have been programmed into them by the world around them. It's not a matter of turning over your will. It's a matter of surrendering your tensions and opening your heart and connecting the divinity that exists within you to the divinity in your teacher.

Why do you wear orange?

My Gurus wore orange, so I wear orange. It is symbolic of the fire of yoga. Some teachers wear white. Orange isn't my best color, but it's easy to find orange T-shirts around here because fortunately it's the Denver Broncos' colors.

The Lineage

Could you tell us about yourself and the lineage of teachers?

In 1970, I was in college in Bloomington, Indiana, and I heard that Swami Rudrananda, a Jewish-American who had been recently given the title of Swami, was coming to give a lecture. I was very interested in spirituality and had heard that he was a powerful and evolved Yogi.

Swami Rudrananda

Rudi, as we call him, came to Bloomington and gave a lecture. As soon as I saw him I said, "That's what I want to be." I don't mean that I wanted to be like him physically or in any other such way. I wanted to attain the state of consciousness that he had. That day, I made my decision to work toward that goal.

He had a little meditation center in Bloomington, but he lived in New York City, so I moved into the Bloomington ashram and began my practice. After a long period of intense practice and sadhana, an in–depth connection was made to

Rudi and the lineage of teachers. To further my work Rudi initiated me as a teacher of Kundalini Yoga. I received his spiritual transmission and his blessing to teach.

After Rudi's death, I later met Swami Muktananda, or Baba, as we call him, who is recognized as one of the great teachers of India. Swami Muktananda and Swami Rudrananda had the same Guru, named Swami Nityananda. Nityananda was a great saint of modern India. Swami Muktananda gave me further instruction and also instructed me to continue my role as a teacher.

It was the quality that I felt in these teachers that drew me to them. I have met many great teachers since my Gurus' death whom I respect very much, but my heart connection is with this lineage of teachers.

Could you tell us about Swami Nityananda?

I never met Swami Nityananda in person. He died before I got to India. But I have felt him profoundly in my life for many, many years. My first experience of Nityananda was with Rudi.

Rudi was talking to people and answering questions, and I was just watching him. After a while, I saw a figure of a very large dark man superimposed on Rudi. It was as if Nityananda was sitting there instead of Rudi. So I began to relate to the connection that Rudi had with Nityananda. When I spent time with Rudi, I began to feel Nityananda in him.

After many years, I went to Ganeshpuri where Nityananda's Samadhi Shrine is. This shrine is where he left his physical body, or took *mahasamadhi*. It was quite extraordinary. I went into the room where his bed was. It was like walking into a room where somebody left the door open to the universe.

The experience was of pure cosmic energy. There was no personality that I could relate to at all. It was just pure energy. Baba Muktananda used to say that Nityananda's energy and consciousness was vast and completely beyond the normal state. I have such a deep love for the connection that he represents. Nityananda is pure grace.

Where did Swami Nityananda come from?

Swami Nityananda was an *Avadhut*, or one who lives constantly in the experience of the Inner Self. He came directly from the realm of the *Avadhuts*. Baba and Rudi were great disciples of Nityananda. They obtained their freedom through their relationship with him. Nityananda was not an ordinary yogi or an ordinary saint. He was very, very special.

What are your experiences of Swami Nityananda?

Nityananda is so vast. My experiences of Nityananda are always almost impossible to put into words. I've felt him and seen him and connected with him on a spiritual level many times, but it always leaves me with an indescribable feeling. When Rudi or Baba taught, they would sometimes turn into Nityananda. Their bodies would disappear and Nityananda would be teaching. I relate to him as the highest principle. Nityananda simply is the Guru Principle.

Nityananda continually lived in the state of *satchitananda*, a state of being beyond words and concepts, a state beyond duality, a state of total freedom. By developing an awareness to this state that he continually radiates, I was able to experience the same state within myself. This is called Guru Yoga. The Guru is not a personality. It is a state of being.

Swami Nityananda

Could you tell us about Baba Muktananda and your relationship with him?

Baba was a great Yogi. I went to him because I felt that he had attained what I was working to attain. I first met him at Miami Beach. There were thousands of people of all religions and races milling around. It was an incredible scene. I asked a friend to introduce me to Baba. He did so at an evening program.

The evening program consisted of a talk, where someone would share his or her experience with Baba, followed by a chant, and then darshan. Darshan is a time when each student can personally meet the teacher and receive his blessing. Baba received each person in a different way. He would talk to some, ignore others, and even yell at some. I had never seen a situation like that. It seemed very foreign.

Baba Muktananda

I was not there to judge or analyze the situation. I was there to learn from the teacher. When I got up to meet Baba, the man I knew jumped up and whispered in

Baba's ear. Baba looked at me for a long time and then waved a fan made of peacock feathers at me. I felt a tremendous rush of energy rising through me – so much so that I felt I would pass out. He gave me another dose of energy with those feathers. I was staggering after the experience. The ushers needed to guide me to my seat.

I sat and tried to absorb the Shakti as best I could. I had been preparing for months to meet Baba. He knew why I was there and gave me what I was looking for. I felt a deep purging take place inside of myself. Since Rudi's death, I had been working for about 10 years on my own. I felt like Baba was purging away all those years of inner excavation.

That evening, a three-day saptah began. A saptah is a long chant that can go on for days or even months. The chant for this saptah was *Hare Krishna*. I was not used to chanting, but did not let that affect my experience. I was there to learn and would not allow anything to come between me and the spiritual nourishment that I knew Baba could supply.

At the time I met Baba, I had two ashrams in Colorado with hundreds of students. I was also a successful businessman. I took all of my students to meet and visit Baba. I felt that he had so much to offer and wanted all my students to benefit from his company.

After the first meeting in Miami Beach, I met him many times in New York. Once I went to visit him for two weeks, thinking that I would be able to spend every evening with him. When I arrived, I was asked to work in the shoe room at the ashram. The people who work in the shoe room are not able to go to the evening darshan program. Although it did not match my expectation of my visit, I worked at that job for several days. I organized the room and helped the others do a better job.

After a few days, Baba asked, "Where is Deepak?" Deepak was the first spiritual name that Baba gave me. It means light.

He was told that I was in the shoe room and immediately sent someone to get me. He had me sit right next to him for the rest of my visit. Baba tested my commitment to my spiritual practice constantly. He wanted to see if I would squander my energy for material success instead of spiritual evolution. I was tested in hundreds of direct and subtle ways. I kept my focus on my practice and tried to imbibe the best that he had to offer. Sometimes he would call me into his private quarters for private darshan. He was so wonderful to me.

Baba had the content and ability to change his students at their core. He was very capable, very functional, and very powerful. He was completely dedicated to pursuing his spiritual growth and attained his realization. Baba and Rudi have stripped away lifetimes of tension from my being with the grace of Swami Nityananda. I owe any success and any development that I might have to my teachers.

When you spoke of Swami Muktananda, you talked about how you felt your karma being burnt up. That was very inspiring to me. I really want that to happen to me.

Muktananda was always willing to help his students grow and evolve. And sometimes, the process of growth is difficult. The teacher is there to facilitate the process. Often people want special attention from the teacher or superficial encouragement. It is better to try to experience the state the teacher has attained and to engage in a relationship at that level. When I went to see Muktananda, I really opened up and I wholeheartedly threw myself into the relationship. I don't know what people are saving themselves for. I feel that when you come in contact with someone who is evolved, if you harmonize and connect with them on a deeper level, there is tremendous potential for growth.

Will you talk about having faith in the teacher?

We all want someone to give us faith. Faith is earned. I can profess all sorts of ideas, but until you have actually taken the teachings and applied them and gotten results, you really won't have much confidence in them. Faith arises when you see the results of your spiritual effort.

My understanding of my Gurus has changed so much. At first, I had resistance to the whole concept of a Guru. My faith grew in them because my practice was bringing results. I was starting to experience the Truth in what they were saying. That made all the difference.

The lineage of teachers at Shoshoni

Painting illustrating the chakras, psychic energy centers, in the body

Chapter Four

The Practice

When your mind is clear through discipline and meditation, you will start to see the true nature of your existence and of everything around you. What you will find is that everything is pure consciousness. It is pure consciousness that permeates all of manifestation.

What is Shambhava Yoga?

The purpose of Shambhava Yoga is to give you an experience of the subtle body, to connect to a deeper level of consciousness, and to function from there. Shambhava Yoga has to do with the unfolding of the energy centers in your subtle body. As you progress in your spiritual evolution, each situation that manifests in life can be used to increase your awareness of the Inner Self.

What is Kundalini meditation?

The Kundalini meditation that I teach is a particular pranayama, or breathing exercise, developed by my teachers. They gave me permission to teach this meditation. The practice is extremely powerful, so I only give it to those students who are ready.

A person shouldn't do this practice unless he or she feels a very strong connection to me and to the Lineage of teachers and is strongly committed to beginning a serious practice. Otherwise, the Kundalini meditation can have a very strong effect and can cause distractions.

Advanced spiritual work isn't a three-week course or a seven-hour intensive. It involves a very deep commitment. When I met Rudi and Baba, I felt something in them. I didn't pay attention to the surroundings. I didn't judge them by their appearance or their philosophy. There was a connection that I felt. And if you feel that, it is something to build on. That's what is important.

A preliminary practice to the Kundalini meditation is the heart meditation, where you learn to work with the energy center in the center of the chest, near the heart. This is the heart meditation technique: breathe in through the nose, and release all thoughts, emotions, and mental activity. Feel them dissolve and melt away. Continue to follow your breath into your heart. Bring the sense of self that you carry in your mind down to your heart by shifting your attention from your mind to your heart. Breathe into your heart center and let go of your desire, definition, and philosophy and simply feel your heart center expand. Hold your attention in your heart as you slowly release your breath.

When you do this practice, you will begin to experience the nature of the energy center in your heart. As you become more and more aware of this center, it will become easier for you to let go of more thoughts, emotions, and obscurations.

Inside of you is a state of being that is totally pure and clear and at peace. While your attention is caught in the movie of the world, that state exists in you. The heart meditation will help you experience this state. It is from that state of clarity that all creativity flows.

What do you mean when you say that we should have a strong spiritual commitment before doing Shambhava Yoga?

I mean that if you are going to do it, you have to be serious about it. And I don't mean serious about doing the actual techniques. You have to be serious about your commitment to grow and change. That is the most important thing. Techniques mean nothing.

You need to have a powerful wish to know the Truth, to find God, and to evolve spiritually. You need the commitment to hang on to the process as it begins to open you up. Many people approach spiritual practice like a person digging a well. One might dig two or three feet here and say, "Oh, it's too rotten. Maybe it's better over here," and then dig two or three feet over there and say, "No, I don't like that spot." The next thing you know, the person never dug deeply enough anywhere. It is important to pick a tradition and a practice and commit yourself to it until you have a realization.

Do you know the Irish story about leprechauns? In Ireland, they say that there are leprechauns who guard a fabulous treasure. They say if you ever see one of these leprechauns, you should grab him by the toe and hang on. First he looks like a leprechaun, then he turns into a terrible dragon, and then a monster, and then a demon. If you let go of the leprechaun, you lose the reward.

This story is symbolic of the kind of a commitment spiritual work takes. As you delve into your own psyche with the exercise, you will be unleashing tendencies and tensions that have accumulated in your psychic system from all your past lives. As you work with the practice, you really have to hang on. Then you get the pot of gold. As you progress in the practice, you will experience an internal state of freedom. You will see that the universe is a manifestation of the play of consciousness.

Is it important to hold your breath as long as possible when doing the heart meditation?

No. It's not good to do it with strong tension or to build tension in the process. It's just a tool. It's not good to strain your system with the Kundalini energy. It should be a gentle process, like watering a plant. The breath comes in, you expand, and the energy soaks in. It's that kind of attention that is required.

Is part of the practice to gather more energy so you can surrender more tension?

It's a way of focusing, drawing in everything and beginning to turn your attention inside, to consciously access these tensions that are on a deeper level. That is what that exercise is for.

The practice feels very heavy sometimes. Am I doing something wrong?

I don't find it heavy! The heaviness that you experience has to do with your inner condition. I remember an analogy Rudi used to make. He said that whereas most people, when they find a nice stream, would build a house by it and make themselves comfortable, a yogi would build a boat to journey upstream.

Certainly you can do a little bit of meditation and a little bit of spiritual work and arrive at a place in life that is fairly peaceful, fairly calm, and fairly smooth. People equate that with spiritual evolvement. But if you look a little deeper into yourself, you will see that there is a little more tension there than you thought.

It is very difficult for me to do the practice. Sometimes I feel like giving up.

Sure, I understand. It's easier to shut down. It takes consciousness, strength of mind, and discipline to grow. The ability to open up to the tensions and fear and resistance that you encounter in yourself and to rise above it is spiritual practice. And it is difficult – sometimes extremely difficult.

Through spiritual work, you begin to have a deeper experience of your real nature. Most people prefer to have an illusion. It's much easier to read a book and fantasize about spirituality than to actually engage in growth.

I don't feel my energy rise when I do the practice. What should I do?

You won't necessarily feel yourself rise when you do the practice. You are asking me for a technique that works immediately. Although there is an immediate benefit to doing the practice, you won't necessarily be aware of the benefit. It is like asking a music teacher, "How can I play Bach?" What could the teacher say? You have to learn to read music and play an instrument. You have to practice for a long time. After some time, you would come to the point in your music practice where you don't expend any effort in reading the music or playing the notes. When that happens, you will be at the point where you can play Bach the way it was meant to be played.

Spiritual work follows the same pattern. You have learned the meditation techniques. It is up to you to practice them and make yourself one with them.

The Experience

Sometimes after doing the practice, I feel as though a hot fire is burning within me. What should I do?

Have a brownie or an ice cream sundae or a cold shower. Don't worry about it. The only reason it feels so intense is because of your contracted state. If you relax more, it won't burn so hot.

The heat is caused by the purification of the energy channels in the subtle body. These channels contain lifetimes of positive and negative experience that block the flow of creative energy through the psychic system. The practice is like Drano for your psychic system. It churns up the tensions in your psyche and allows for purification to take place.

During meditation, I feel a very powerful surge of energy in my forehead which gets stronger and moves to my ears. My ears start ringing. What should I do? What is going on?

Just keep opening and allow that to happen. The ringing in your ears is the Kundalini Shakti moving through your body. In the subtle body, there are energy pathways that connect your energy centers. As your system becomes more purified and sensitive, you will begin to hear the vibration of the purified energy moving through your nervous system. So just relax and go with what is happening and let it express itself.

Why don't meditators have similar experiences?

We are all human beings, and we are all structured in similar ways. But we do not have the same set of past experiences. When we begin our practice, our past experience affects our experience during meditation. But after a period of time, when the practice becomes deeper, certain signs manifest that are the same for everyone.

What are those signs?

It's best that I don't mention them. Sometimes people cheat and try to make them happen. When something happens to you, ask me and I'll tell you what it means. Many people try to have the experience of these higher states of consciousness without doing the groundwork. To develop a groundwork, one needs to practice diligently. I had been meditating for at least eight to ten years before I knew that the experiences I was having were documented in many Indian and Tibetan scriptures. After I met Baba, he said I should read the scriptures to understand the experiences. But I had the experiences first and then I read about them – not the other way around. It's best to practice regularly with devotion and commitment.

Could you tell me something about involuntary body movements?

They are called kriyas, which means action in Sanskrit. As your psychic system unfolds, you may experience mental, emotional, or physical kriyas. They are no problem. It is a natural process. Sometimes as the purification process takes place, you might experience some shaking in your physical body. Instead of trying to control them, just relax and breath into them.

Why do I feel so rigid sometimes?

That's all right. Sometimes the rigidity that you feel is not because of something happening to you in the external world.

It's a condition that you are uncovering in yourself. When you feel the rigidity coming up, bring the practice into play, burn it up, transcend it, and open up your system again. That's called spiritual work.

When you do spiritual work, you grow. When you grow, you uncover deeper and deeper things. Often, people want to be better and more fulfilled inside, but they want someone else to magically remove all their problems. But these problems are lodged very tightly in the psychic system. It takes a very concerted effort with discipline and consciousness to loosen very deep tensions. You can't open the door to your psychic system unless you have the key. The key is consciousness, discipline, and energy.

I feel tremendous surges of the Kundalini energy through my body during my day. What is going on?

As Kundalini starts to move through your subtle body, you may feel powerful surges of energy. The balls of my feet used to vibrate! Just keep doing the practice through your day. I would find myself in all sorts of very mundane situations in the physical plane while a very profound spiritual transformation was taking place in my psychic system. That is very good. Don't try to rarefy your spiritual life. Sometimes people try to isolate their spiritual life and run away from the world. If you can go through the internal process in the midst of your day-to-day life, then it's wonderful. It will make what is happening to you very real and very strong. I went through very powerful experiences when I first started Kundalini Yoga. It would make a funny movie.

Last night I felt as though I had left my body. Could you explain what I was feeling?

When the energy centers in your subtle body reach a certain level of vibration, your Self separates from the physical self. People often feel tremendous fear at that point because it feels like they are dead or about to die. It's no problem.

What should I have done?

Just relax and surrender. It is not so easy to turn off the body. You don't have to worry about it so much. Besides if you actually leave and don't come back, you've graduated! But that is not likely to happen. When you have these experiences in the subtle realm, the mind takes this experience and projects it a certain way. Just keep relaxing your mind and don't get too attached to the manifestation. The manifestation we perceive in these other states isn't necessarily the Truth of what is going on. It is an interpretation. The more you can relax the mind, the less manifestation will occur, because your emotions won't get so tangled up in it.

Before one is established in that state, is it better to avoid situations that create a lot of tension?

It is important to be very conscious about the decisions that you make. I'm talking from my own experience. Because when I was young, I had more energy than sense. That gave me a great deal of difficulty.

I learned to allow my life to unfold rather than try to manipulate it with my will. When you start to manipulate the world around you with your will, you're just expressing desire and you are creating karma. This will have its ramifications. The more stabilized you are in the practice, the freer you become. You will be more expansive and will be able to easily encompass more and more of life.

Somebody who is really evolved and growing spiritually should be able to function in any situation. That's been my experience and the experience of my teachers. It's just like a great chef. A great chef who needs a bunch of very expensive and special ingredients to make a meal is not really a great chef. A great chef is one who can use the ingredients at hand to make a fine meal. In the same way, people who are spiritually evolving don't need special conditions in which to grow. Whatever conditions they find themselves in are the right conditions.

I have an energy block in my system. It becomes very painful during meditation. What can I do to help this?

As you are meditating, go to where that block is and really work to surrender above it. It's a matter of putting your attention there and in a sense releasing it. The blocks that we have are caused by energy under pressure. Simple physical pain can be neutralized by expanding your energy. Put your attention above the pain and allow everything to flow through. It will remove all sorts of blocks.

Everyone wants to feel good all the time, and it's totally immature and unrealistic. If you find some place where they say you don't have to do anything and you'll feel nothing but bliss all the time, you've found your death. It's through the challenges of our life that we grow and evolve. The ability to open up to your life and transcend it is a sign of real spiritual maturity and development. People who only look for pleasant experiences are going to have a lot of trouble in this world.

Sometimes I feel tremendous anger after doing the practice. Why is that?

There is a great deal of emotion and tension stored in your psychic system. And as you start to open up, you have to be responsible to work with the practice. Because when you start to open up your psychic system, you are starting to unleash a lot of pent-up energy. You have to become more responsible and more conscious in how you live your life and how you act.

At the moment you feel the anger arise, the appropriate way to work is to breathe into your heart and expand yourself to the point where the anger dissolves. When you can do that consciously, when you can take an emotion or some other strong energy and transmute it into a very positive energy that moves through your psychic system, then you are making some progress.

That's what I mean by "consciousness." It is not a matter of how long you sit and meditate, but it is the awareness and the consciousness that you bring to all the elements that are a part of your day that really determine whether you grow or not.

Everybody wants somebody else to do it for them. We will pay any amount of money to go to a doctor or healer to make all the pain we feel go away. You have to take responsibility for it and you have to begin to work on it. Where there is effort, there is grace. Enlightened beings such as Swami Nityananda provide grace even without their physical presence. They supply the support and the energy necessary to nourish and sustain you while you develop the consciousness to transcend your limitations.

That is why in spiritual work it is so important that you have a teacher. It isn't something that you can just read in a book and learn in six weeks or six months or six years. It is a process that will take you completely to your freedom. So once you have started practicing in earnest, every situation is an opportunity to grow. When strong emotions come out or even strong doubt or strong fears, you have to begin to see that this is part of your spiritual growth, and apply the practice. Then you will start to grow spiritually.

Many people wonder if they are doing the practice right. You are doing it correctly if you slowly begin to transcend your patterns. It is not a matter of looking for anger or looking for negative feelings or looking for fear. They come by themselves. If you spend three days getting over something when you first start the practice, after you have been practicing for a while, you should be able to get over it in three seconds and move on.

We spend an enormous amount of time replaying painful experiences through our head and blaming people for our situation. If you are stuck in that state of mind, you will never evolve spiritually. You are wasting all your energy on the horizontal, emotional, material level. But working through such experiences brings tremendous growth. It brings tremendous inner depth.

I find that as I progress in the practice, I get very emotional. What advice do you have for me?

Keep approaching your tensions and fears. Most people would rather do anything than to open up to that part of themselves. And it is just that part of themselves – that fear, that anger, or whatever emotion it might be – that blocks the flow of creative energy.

To really grow and evolve as a human being you need to have the courage to keep approaching, in a very direct way, these areas of tension and transcend them. The first time you do this, it can be quite terrifying. After that, it is fun.

In the 35 years that I have been meditating, I have never had any experience before coming here. Yesterday my experience was so strong that I started to cry.

That's a purification of your psychic system. When your psychic system starts to open and you have a glimmer of the Self, it can be overwhelming. When I went to see Baba for the first time, I cried for four days. It wasn't out of sadness; it was something awakening in me.

Shaktipata

Could you discuss energy transmission? What is that and what does it mean?

The practice of yoga that we do here has the ability to awaken the dormant Kundalini energy in a person. Everyone has a spark of divinity and pure consciousness within them, but it is usually encased in accumulated tensions and unconsciousness and karma. The specialty of my Gurus is to awaken this energy within the student.

The process is called *Shaktipata*, and it's as simple as lighting one candle with another. There is a divine consciousness within each human being that has created the manifestation of the whole universe. We can be fully aware of this divinity, or Inner Self. During our lives, we accumulate experiences that block our awareness of the Inner Self. When you meditate with someone who is conscious of this state and who can transmit energy, you can gain an experience of your own Self. It's not like anyone is doing anything to you; it's more like somebody is showing you where the light switch is so you can become more aware of this consciousness.

On one level there is a great deal of mystery about *Shaktipata*. But on another level it is really simple. Ultimately the benefit you derive from this experience has to do with your own effort, understanding, and practice.

I was wondering how you felt when you left last night after giving Shaktipata?

I felt pretty good. At times it can be tiring, but that depends on my condition. It took me quite a while to get to sleep; my toes were vibrating. What I am doing is sharing with everyone something that was given to me by my teachers. I was instructed to share it with anyone and everyone who shows up.

After I received Shaktipata, I felt as though I was already enlightened. I am wondering whether this is just my mind going a bit crazy on the Shakti.

In a sense, you are already enlightened. The enlightened state exists inside you and everyone else. You do not need to search for your enlightenment – you just need to recognize it. Shaktipata gives you a spontaneous recognition of your Inner Self. The problem is that the mind starts to interpret the Shaktipata experience, instead of just resting in it. As you meditate and become more stabilized in the practice, your awareness of your true n ature will increase.

Baba said that enlightenment exists between the inhalation and the exhalation, between *Ham* and *Sah* in the *Ham Sah* mantra. If you do that practice, you will find a moment where everything stops. Your mind stops, your breath stops, and everything disappears. That is the state of Samadhi, or enlightenment. So certainly everyone has had an experience of that some time or another. It comes in many different ways. The trick is to become established in that state.

I used to sit with Baba and Rudi and experience a state that was extraordinarily profound. When I would leave, I would fall back into my own state of consciousness. But their company inspired me to find that state in myself. People have a Hollywood view of what enlightenment is, with all its definitions, expectations, and concepts that don't have much reality. The more you grow spiritually the clearer your mind becomes. The world becomes a simple place.

Conscious Sleep

What is the nature of sleep?

For most people, sleep is an unconscious state. Those who are adept at meditation can experience a state beyond sleep called the turiya state. They are not unconscious during sleep. They don't lose awareness of their true nature in the waking, dreaming, or sleep state. They are conscious through all of these states.

I've experienced a state that is between sleep and wakefulness. I find that I often contemplate on that state.

Don't spend time pondering your experience. Let your experience go and keep going deeper. If you want to contemplate something, you might follow the example of the Buddhists who contemplate impermanence. Contemplating impermanence will bring you to the understanding that everything is impermanent.

Does meditation reduce your need for sleep?

I've gone through periods when it has reduced my need for sleep. But there are other times when I am working very deeply that I find I need more rest. The physical body is limited, but the spirit is unlimited. You can make great spiritual strides while sleeping.

I would like to know how to increase my awareness while sleeping. What instruction do you have?

Begin by following the breath as you inhale and exhale. As you exhale, instead of allowing your attention to go outside with the exhalation, keep it in your heart center. And if your mind becomes agitated or distracted use the *Ham Sah* mantra.

This is an opportunity to open up to a new level in yourself and to connect with something a little deeper than you've experienced before. People often go to sleep with their minds rather unfocused. They replay thoughts and "movies" from their lives. Try and go to sleep consciously. Let your inhalation draw in energy and nourishment and allow your exhalation to let go of your tensions. Relax and try to have a sense of surrender. Keep your attention focused in your heart. If you are aware that you are dreaming, if you can be a witness to your dreams rather than being propelled by them, then you can even do the practice while dreaming

If done correctly, you will experience a different level of consciousness in your sleep. Sleep is an opportunity to grow if you approach it consciously. Try tonight. Try to relax and surrender consciously into your sleep.

Are dreams significant?

People consider their dreams to be very significant. But a dream is only as valuable as the clarity and steadiness of your mind. You have to have a clear and steady mind to be able to access the unconscious and get reliable information. If you can keep your mind steady and clear, then even while you are awake ideas will bubble up that have meaning and will give you guidance and direction.

But if your mind uncontrollably swings with your emotions and circumstances, then dreams are pretty unreliable. So don't worry about your dreams or get too attached to them. Just let them go and work for a steady, clear state of consciousness. That's what meditation brings about.

Since I started feeling Kundalini energy, I have had many bad dreams.

Bad dreams usually reflect fears that you have. When one starts the process of inner awakening through Shambhava Yoga, the obscurations or obstacles that are carried in the psychic system will surface.

In medicine, you are sometimes given a little bit of the disease as an antidote. Shambhava Yoga is similar in that certain things will be stirred up in your psychic system that may make you a little uncomfortable. If, at this point, you use your understanding of the practice to continue opening your system, you can be freed of many obstacles.

We have a tendency to stop or avoid negative emotions when they arise, rather than opening up and letting them go. Letting go is the correct way to work with these negativities. In most cases, our obstacles have been part of our psychic systems for a very long time, and we don't want to let go of them. I have found that people are attached to the things that cause them pain and suffering more than anything else.

Relationships

Do I need to avoid romantic relationships to evolve spiritually?

No. Just open your heart and surrender and keep your attention focused on your spiritual practice and your growth. What comes to you when you are in that state is your karma. Your karma is nothing more than an opportunity to free yourself of an illusion and to go beyond the previous patterns that you might have set up.

The experience we are searching for in relationships is the experience of inner contentment and inner happiness. As you do the practice, you will start to have that experience inside you, independent of whether you are with someone or not.

I'm curious as to what words you would have to offer to a broken heart.

I would ask whose heart is broken. And keep asking. Don't accept the first 2,000 answers! I've had my heart broken many times until I figured out what was breaking. The end of a relationship can be used as a catalyst to make a leap to a new level of awareness.

When your heart is broken, and your world is destroyed, the illusion you have created is exposed. If you can simply step through it, everything changes. But unfortunately, we just try to reconstruct it based upon the debris of the previous illusion. The foundation gets shakier and shakier over time because the material has less and less reality to it.

Could you talk a little about the advantages and disadvantages of having a partner who is doing the same spiritual practice as you?

There is no advantage or disadvantage. Each has its own limitations. People think that they are going to do their "spiritual work together," but ultimately it is the individual's effort that matters. Each person has to do his or her own work.

Sexual Energy

Could you discuss sexual energy?

Sexual energy is just another powerful energy that exists in your body. It takes maturity and depth of practice to understand what role sexuality plays in life. Most people don't understand their sexuality very well. Through past sexual experiences, they know that it is a pleasant activity, but have no idea about the deeper process underlying their sexuality. That takes a certain level of inner discipline to understand.

If you can't keep your mind still and focused, the sexual energy is very difficult to master. The best way to work with sexual energy is to observe its effect on your psychic system. If you can do that, you will have transcended the unconscious patterns of sexual expression. If you can absorb the sexual energy into your psychic system through your energy centers, you will get a deeper understanding of your sexuality.

In the West, there is very little understanding of how to deal with sexual energy. Most people try to indulge in sexual activity as much as they can until it is not fun anymore. Then they seek out someone else with whom the sex is even better. Many people just leap from person to person without ever understanding their own sexual drive. Understanding the drive is the key element to mastering sexuality.

There is nothing wrong with sex. The basic question is: does the sexual energy control you or are you in control of it? If you are in control of that energy, then sex can become a subtle and refined art form. If you are a victim of it, then you are just rolling around in the mud thinking you are having a good time. You won't go to hell if you have too much sex, but you might deplete yourself of a great deal of energy.

Are you referring to Tantric sex?

Most people don't understand the idea of Tantric sex. They think it has to do with physical activities rather than controlling energy. Tantric sex requires a very high level of skillfulness and discipline to control your subtle energy. And only when you attain a level of mastery can it have any effect.

Most sexual activity usually boils down to an exchange of energies at a very unconscious level. People think that as long as they feel good after sex, the activity was beneficial. That level of unconsciousness makes the experience a total waste. Being able to conserve, control, and discipline your sexual energy can give you an opportunity to make tremendous advancements on an inner level. But if you have no discipline and are a victim of your own desires, you will never understand Tantra.

Is celibacy necessary for spiritual growth?

Some people can be celibate, and others cannot. The question is not whether you are celibate or not, it's whether or not you are in control of your energy. There are some people who are celibate who aren't in control of their energy. It would be terrible to be celibate and spend all your time thinking about nothing but sex.

When you have mastered your sexuality, you will find that sex is not such a big deal. Understanding your own sexuality means that you see how it controls you, how it motivates you, how it defines you, how it colors everything you see. When you have gained some inner experience, then you can separate and see all that very clearly. But imposing something on yourself that has nothing to do with your karma or your stage of evolution is a problem. Just start from where you are now. I know many great masters who were celibates and others who were householders. It's the subtle understanding of sexual energy that is important to grasp.

When sexual energy surfaces during meditation, what should I do?

Try to circulate the energy through your psychic system. Basically, if you feel energy in any energy center, just keep opening and expanding it. Ultimately, the highest expression of the sexual energy is union with the Self.

I find that sexual energy is surfacing in me when I do the practice.

We experience the world through our five senses, and they define our view of reality. As you experience these energies rising in you, try to go to their source. If you can turn your attention on the source of the energy, you'll break through the need to express it on the physical level.

You will begin to understand how to use the sexual energy in a much more conscious way. The sexual energy perpetuates the human race and perpetuates our level of manifestation, so it is a powerful energy. Most people are victims of their sexuality; either they express it without consciousness or they suppress it. Suppression of a desire is not the same as being free from it. It will inevitably surface in some other manner.

Having a deep inner life should allow you to be clearer and freer in everything you do, and to find more creative capacity and a deeper sense of connection to your life. The point is not to reject your sexuality, but to transcend it.

Swami at his Shoshoni Yoga Retreat Center

Chapter Five

Transcending Experience

You do not need to search for your enlightenment. You just need to recognize it. If you could direct your attention fully inside and experience the pure consciousness which is the foundation of your entire being, you will recognize your true state. Everyone has experienced a spontaneous recognition of their true nature at different times. When the Inner Self flashes forth, we immediately attribute the experience to an external attachment and are again caught in the wheel of samsara.

How can I have a tenderness of heart and at the same time maintain the attitude of a warrior while I am working in the world? I find that I am either too hard or too soft.

In the midst of your battle, you have to stop and smell the roses. You should have a warrior's spirit when it comes to dealing with your mind, emotions, resistance, and tensions. But while doing that, you should have loving compassion for the people you interact with. We usually have the greatest compassion for our own suffering, and we abuse everyone else. So the simple, practical answer to that is before you open your mouth, you open your heart.

The Work Place

Can you give me any advice for working in the material world?

While you are in the midst of your activity, draw your attention inside. You will find that the activity that you are performing gets easier. If you internalize your awareness and access the flow of Shakti, your capacity for spiritual work as well as material work will increase dramatically. The mind is the obstacle because it has the sense of doership and a sense of limitation. It is not a matter of "working harder" in the way that phrase is usually interpreted. Just focus your attention inside. The mind is a very powerful and useful tool, but if it is twisted with desire, even the desire for self-improvement, it can not function as it was meant to function. A person who has developed a steady mind is usually very creative. Such a person does not see problems – only solutions.

How can I use the practice while working in the business world?

It's no problem. You need to develop the capacity to use the dramatic, tense situations that you encounter in life which can create anxiety, fear, and anger to rise spiritually.

I don't just hide out in a cave all the time. I can function in virtually any kind of situation. I make conscious decisions about my activities, but if I had to I can still go and cook in a restaurant and wash dishes. I don't need a rarefied atmosphere to function on a spiritual level. People think freedom is having enough money, time, and circumstances to do all the things that they put off doing because they had children and careers. And they say, "I can't wait to be free." And then after they retire, they go nuts when they don't have anything to do.

Freedom is the ability to function through any circumstance, whether it be painful or pleasant, from the state of pure consciousness and clarity. That state is discovered through meditation. That's real freedom. My teacher, Rudi, was incredible. He lived in midtown Manhattan and was an Oriental art dealer. Every maniac in New York City at one time or another came walking through his little store. In the midst of the chaos of the city, he was able to completely identify with the state of pure clarity and pure awareness.

Baba Muktananda was the same way. It didn't matter whether he was talking to prime ministers or to villagers. He was always immersed in the state of spiritual intoxication. That's a sign of spiritual evolvement. A person who needs special circumstances in which to function is spiritually handicapped.

I have a situation at work that has become adversarial. Do you have any advice?

When you transcend a situation energetically, and your mind is clear and not defensive, or plotting or scheming, you have the ability to handle the situation better. I have dealt with some pretty heavyweight competitive personalities, so I know what I am talking about. If you try to meet them on the same energetic level, you won't always succeed. There is always someone stronger who can overwhelm you. But if you can emotionally, mentally, and energetically get above a situation, your competitors cannot lay a glove on you. Meditation does not make a person unclear or unconscious. As you progress, the outer world does not change that much. It is the inner experience that changes. If I cannot feel very positive about a person, I at least try to feel neutral. And I've been challenged. It is just a skillful way for living in the world. The whole purpose of Shambhava Yoga is not to reject the world. The purpose is to learn how to function skillfully in the world so that you can use each experience to rise spiritually.

How can I function from a state of clarity when I am at work?

You have to learn how to harmonize with the situation energetically. When I used to work in the business world, while I was in the midst of the most tension-filled situations, I would use the Kundalini practice to rise above the tension of the situation. I learned to take the very coarse and gross energy of a tense situation and use it to raise my internal energy level. I tried to rise above whatever reaction I felt within myself.

When I say "rising above," I mean that my mind and emotions were not involved in the situation. I was dancing, in a sense, with the situation rather than attacking it in a combative way. It's like a ballet of energy. In that way, I can maintain a state of clarity under virtually all circumstances. That's what inner consciousness allows you to do in the outer world. But when you are coming from a posture of attack and defense, life inevitably becomes a battle. I didn't learn these techniques by sitting in a cave or sitting in my room meditating for 14 hours a day. I learned it by bringing my spiritual practice into my daily life. So when I was dealing with financiers and lawyers, I was focusing inside myself. When I was near the verge of bankruptcy, I was working inside, and when I was a successful businessman, I was working inside. That is real practice of Shambhava Yoga.

How can I keep my psychic system open while working in the outside world? I tend to shut down in negative atmospheres.

It takes discrimination. You wouldn't go to a nightclub and sit there and meditate and try to absorb the atmosphere, would you? On the other hand, when you are in a positive atmosphere, such as this ashram, you can open yourself up and begin to work spiritually.

A person doing this practice does not energetically connect to negative situations. Instead, the person circulates the Kundalini energy upward, toward the highest energy centers. In that sense, the person does not connect with the negative situation. The person's energy is quite literally above the situation. On the external level there is neither acceptance nor rejection of the negative situation.

We attract particular situations because there is a tension inside of us that can relate to the situation. So when you attract a situation in the external world, you can dissolve your attachment to it internally through surrender and transcendence. In this way, you are purging yourself of that particular level of expression. If there is no attachment left to that level of expression, you are free of it. You are one step closer to your enlightenment.

From the yogic point of view, it is not a matter of rejecting the world. It is a matter of learning how to survive it skillfully. There are many different levels of spiritual work. When you begin, you are working on the horizontal plane. When the Kundalini is awakened, you develop the ability to work on a vertical plane. What you find is that it is possible to draw energy from the horizontal plane to ascend the vertical plane.That is the nature of Kundalini Yoga.

I am trying to do my spiritual work, but it sometimes seems that I am only blocking out negative situations.

Don't block the negativity out. When you find yourself in situations that have diverse energy, instead of putting blinders on and trying to escape, try to encompass the diversity of the situation. Try to expand beyond it. This is Tantra, which is the science and practice of encompassing diverse energies from real situations. Instead of being judgmental or distracted by situations in life, try to use them to raise your own level of awareness and consciousness.

The scriptures say that a yogi neither accepts nor rejects. That is a formula for working with energy of a situation. The understanding gained from that practice is very real and very powerful.

As my energy increases internally, I find that my outer life becomes more complex. What is going on?

Yes, that often happens. You are spending your energy in the outer world rather than using it to grow spiritually. You have to make conscious decisions so that you can use your energy to grow. People think that if they accumulate experiences on the material level, they are growing spiritually, but that doesn't have much to do with spiritual development.

When you have a very dynamic situation on the material level, it indicates a high energy flow. As you do the Kundalini practice, you will develop the capacity to be energetically above the situations that you attract in life. The process is not a rejection of life. It is a transmutation of the raw experiences of life into refined energy.

I feel my life is pushing me to my limit. It is a little scary.

When I felt near the edge, I used it as a catalyst. You have to learn how to use everything, even your fear, to really motivate you for spiritual growth. Fear is just energy under pressure. Find out where the fear is in your psychic system and use the Shakti to break it down to a flow.

Family

Do you have any advice for raising children?

The condition and quality of your mind has the greatest impact on your children. If you are in a fearful, paranoid, or some other negative condition, it will impact your child accordingly. However, if your heart is open and filled with loving compassion, and you can transcend difficult situations with clarity and balance, your child will develop the same capacities. So it is how you live, how conscious you are that has the effect on them.

With these capacities, no matter what your child's karma might be, he or she will have the content, the consciousness, the pattern, so to speak, to deal with it. That is the way you can really help your child.

I feel that much of my negativity is due to my parents. I feel that if I love them more, it might help my situation.

Well, that is a good direction – but that's psychology. It's not going to solve the basic problem. To do that, you need to energetically open up to the tension and circulate the Shakti through that. In my experience, that works.

Do you have some advice for dealing with negative family situations?

If you are interacting with them through your mind and emotions and a mental sense of openness, you will get tremendously drained. If you can find your Inner Self, not the small self that is so and so and does such and such, but the higher consciousness in you and relate to those people from that state, you can be of tremendous benefit. You won't get exhausted or ripped off. You have to get out of your emotions. You have to find your spiritual connection and function from there in difficult situations. Whenever I meet someone that drains my energy, I don't spend time trying to analyze or judge or attack the person who brought up the negative feeling. I'm more interested in removing the negativity from myself so that I am free of that particular kind of psychic tension. Because in freeing myself of that psychic tension, I'm fulfilling my karma. The negativity that I experienced was simply uncovered by the person. The negativity is in me – not in the other person.

When you become free of these kinds of negativities, it does not mean that the people who bring up the negativities disappear. Instead, they don't have the ability to draw any negativity out of you. In that sense, you are free of them.

Do you have any advice for dealing with very difficult situations?

The best thing you can do in a difficult situation is to stay above it. If you work at the same level of the situation, you won't have the same effect as if you were above it. What I mean by "being above the situation" is that you are not responding to the situation from a place of anger or fear. You are dealing with it from a state of internal quietness. Keep your mind stable, centered, and balanced. Stay above the particular display that is going on. Approaching a difficult situation in this way sucks the energy right out of it. If you start interacting with the situation with your limited sense of self, you will just feed it. If you want to change a situation, you have to transcend it. That means that you lose your attachment and your aversion, and deal with it from a very clear mind. It really works! You can magically change a situation by being above it. If you are underneath, it you get beaten up.

The situations that we attract in our life are all reflections of tensions and karma that we are carrying in our own psychic system. We think that by quitting our difficult job and leaving difficult relationships our life will get better. If you are at all objective, you will see the patterns repeat themselves over and over again. It is either that the world is full of people who are out to get you or there is something wrong with the way you are reading the situation. People who are really involved in growth attract and encompass more and more. Obstacles become nothing more than fuel for their further development. A person who doesn't have that understanding sees the world as a painful place, and they are always trying to maneuver themselves into a situation where difficulties don't exist.

But you can never run away from obstacles, because they are a part of the baggage you carry inside of you. Growth comes by simply sitting down and surrendering all of the tensions that you feel during your life.

If I find myself in an emotionally heavy situation with my family, should I work with the Kundalini energy to break down the heaviness?

There is no fixed formula. Sometimes it is enough to be detached from the situation. Other times it is necessary to consciously work with the breath to grind up the tensions.

There is no cookbook recipe for growth. It has to do with the situation, your condition, and your level of energy. Our parents and family are very important links in our psychic chain. We have to resolve our karma with them if we are ever going to break free of the wheel of samsara. You can't escape your family; you're carrying them inside you.

What is the difference between being detached and being indifferent?

A detached person is not psychically or emotionally drawn into a situation. For example, think about how a surgeon works. If a surgeon is emotionally involved with the pain of the patient, the surgeon will not perform as well as if he or she were detached. The surgeon definitely cares for the patient and has no feelings of indifference. In the same way, a person who is detached can be of great help in difficult situations.

Why is the world so distracting?

It is the nature of samsaric existence. Our predispositions drive us to our life experience. With a little bit of consciousness and effort, you free yourself of your predispositions and live life in a different way. It is not a matter of rejecting the world. It's a matter of not being mesmerized by it.

The world is a good place. It is a good place to free yourself of everything that separates you from your inner experience. You don't have to reject the world; you just have to understand its nature and transcend it.

You can easily get above the distractions, unless you have emotion and desire and attachment. Then, it is a little harder to have that separation take place. As one becomes more and more bound by the pressures the world brings, the person usually ends up totally submerged in it. Don't judge yourself too harshly. Use the practice and allow it to work for you.

Material Desires

I desire some things very much. Should I work to surrender the attachment, or should I work to draw those things into my life and then surrender my attachment?

It works both ways. Sometimes you will do the practice and surrender your attachment and then you will obtain the object that you surrendered. Then, if you are working correctly, you will wonder why in the world you ever wanted it. And then you can let it go. If you are fortunate and able to work very effectively spiritually, you can see into the illusion and the nature of your attachment, and not have to manifest your desire.

If you set a very high goal for yourself, such as attaining liberation, and you stay focused on it, everything that you ever wanted comes. The objects of your desire manifest so that you can see them for what they are and be through with them.

Rudi once said anyone can give up possessions that they never had. But to possess something and then transcend your attachment is real freedom. People are full of desires, and they often accumulate the objects of their desire. But if you look clearly, you'll find that people are never satisfied with their accumulation. It just leads to more desire and more accumulation.

When I was young, I had many desires. My greatest desire was to attain a spiritual realization. I really wanted to be enlightened because, at the age of 21, I looked around me and I kept saying, "What is the point of all this?" When you open up to your life that way, whatever you have to accomplish is attracted to you. If you chase after things, they don't come any faster.

After many years of working, it is much easier not to have to go through getting objects of desire. I can dissolve the attachment before the manifestation. This is much better, but it takes a great deal of energy and consciousness. So you have to start where you are at. Developing discrimination takes time.

But if I don't pursue anything in the outside world, am I not being passive?

No, no. I have never sat back and been passive in my life. I had to feed myself, house myself, and make a living. So I created Rudi's Restaurant and many other businesses. But I never let those become an obstacle in my spiritual growth. Eventually, I transcended my attachment to those things.

We find ourselves in certain situations in life. It is from those situations that we attract our life experience. Don't ever let it be an obstacle or let it consume all your energy. A person who is growing spiritually will become more skillful in working with energy. As your desires diminish, your energy flow increases, and more of life comes to you.

So if I have a desire, I understand that I should watch how it affects me and then bring the practice into play.

Exactly. Use your practice to deal with it.

When you say "use your practice," what I understand is that I circulate the Kundalini energy and expand my energy centers when the desire arises. Am I right?

Yes. That is the way to work spiritually and the essence of

Kundalini Yoga. That is how to consciously work with energy. If you feel something arise in you that has a powerful pull on you, deal with it by opening yourself up to the desire. That does not mean that you indulge in the desire. It means that you open up beyond it and learn how to work with that tension in yourself until you can transcend it. This is the practice of Tantra. If you can transcend the attachment once, you can develop the capacity to live above that level of desire continuously. If you do it once, you can do it all the time.

Often people will transcend an attachment and then get sucked back into it. I see it in people's relationships all the time. They attract a relationship that is bad for them because it rips them off energetically. They finally get rid of it and reaccumulate some energy. When their energy level is about to change, they attract the same kind of person and another stupid relationship. It is an endless cycle.

There is nothing outside of you that is going to change that pattern. It is the consciousness, the awareness, and the clarity of mind that you develop in yourself to see these patterns which will be the foundation for your practice. The ability to apply the practice under all circumstances is the key to liberation.

When I feel that I have transcended a pattern, I still remember it, but I am not caught by it.

Right. You never forget your patterns. If you can transcend a pattern for one second today, tomorrow you will be able to transcend it for two seconds. The process of growth is gradual. A tree does not become a tree overnight. It takes time to sink its roots in the mud and reach for the heat of the sun.

If you can bring yourself above the level of a particular pattern, that doesn't mean that the pattern is magically gone forever. Some things take a while. Some take lifetimes. Once you can live above it, you are not reinforcing the pattern. You are not feeding the pattern; you have put it on a diet. And through your lack of feeding the pattern, eventually the pattern just shrivels up and drops away. There will be so much momentum and so much growth that you really won't notice.

Death and Rebirth

What are you supposed to focus on at the time of death?

Place your attention on the deepest experience of your Inner Self. For me, it is very easy. I just put my attention on Nityananda. I can hold my attention on him very clearly in my mind for a long time. Let's put it this way. If you have no mental or inner discipline, if you don't know how to deal with fear or pain, or if you don't understand detachment and surrender, you will try to cling to the things that were important to you in the material world. Unless you have built a real inner capacity to keep surrendering and connecting to the Inner Self and have a relationship to that, your death might be quite frightening.

You have to rely on your own inner consciousness. No matter what you attain in this life or how much you accomplish, at the moment of your death it is the amount of your spiritual consciousness that makes all the difference. All your attachments will be an anchor or, with the help of a spiritual practice, a source of energy that will free you into a whole other dimension.

What is the cycle of death and rebirth in spiritual work?

In spiritual growth there is always a cycle of death and rebirth. If you are involved with a serious practice you will open up to new areas in your being and release certain kinds of energies. There will be a new level. There are endless new levels.

As you progress in the work, you accumulate enough energy to attain another level. The process of moving from one level to another is very similar to the process of death and rebirth. If you are unconscious about this process, you can spend a long time in the death cycle. It is the unconsciousness with which we live our life that prevents us from experiencing the Self.

Swami Rudrananda (Rudi)

Chapter Six
FREEDOM

Freedom does not arise from obtaining possessions. It is an internal state that is unaffected by the fluctuations of the mind. A free person neither accepts nor rejects life experience and lives in complete union with the Self.

I have an insatiable desire to be free. How should I proceed?

When you feel the burning desire in your heart for spiritual freedom, fan the flames with spiritual practice. Your karma will rush at you, and you will have to transcend it without getting tangled up. It is the clarity of mind that meditation brings that shows you the true nature of your existence. If freedom and happiness existed in the material world, everyone would attain it.

Most people identify freedom as having the money and the circumstances to do whatever they want. That is not real freedom. Freedom is a condition when everything is surrendered. When you have nothing left to lose, you are free. You are free when, regardless of your circumstances, regardless of your life situation, you are totally immersed in the experience of the Self.

Look at people who obtain the "perfect career," or the "perfect relationship," or the "perfect child," with the idea of attaining happiness and spiritual freedom. Are they free? Are they happy? Are they fulfilled? Chances are, your answer is "no." If freedom doesn't exist in the material world then where does it exist? It exists in your ability to attain a deep level of awareness of your true nature. That is the last place anyone wants to look, but that is where it exists. People are caught up in the struggle of attaining and accumulating possessions and experiences on the material level with the hope of finding some balance, some happiness, or some satisfaction. When they have a material attainment and it doesn't satisfy their inner desire, they usually try to obtain a different possession in order to fill their internal desire. It is a cycle of external pursuit, attainment, and discontent.

What are the qualities of a free person?

A truly free person lives in the realization of the Inner Self, a state that exists untainted by the external world and within everyone. We are a product of this climate, this culture, and this soil. Crazy as the world might seem, and distracting as it might be, we have to learn how to maintain an inner consciousness and an inner awareness in the midst of our life experience. That is the essence of Kundalini Yoga, of what I am doing, and of what I teach.

Nityananda, a divine saint

Acknowledgments & Addresses

The editor gratefully acknowledges the help of Miryam Jaffe and Rudrani Tooth for transcribing Swami's question and answer sessions, and Jagdish Srivastava for his valuable comments. The portraits of Swami Rudrananda and Baba Muktananda are courtesy of Wendell Field, and the photographs in the interior and back cover of the book are courtesy of Faith Stone. The photography on the cover is courtesy of Gary the Photographer.

The Shambhava School of Yoga has two main centers in the U.S.A. In addition, there are ashrams and centers in Adelaide, Australia, and Norwich, England, as well as various centers throughout the U.S.

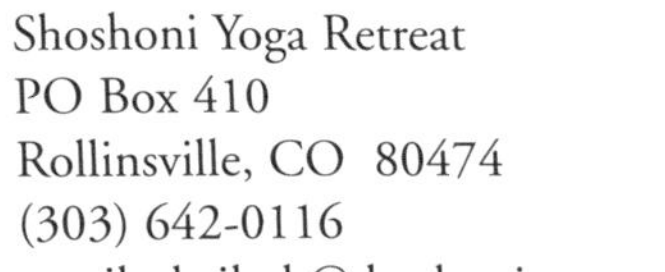

Shoshoni Yoga Retreat
PO Box 410
Rollinsville, CO 80474
(303) 642-0116
email: kailash@shoshoni.org
web site: http://www.shoshoni.org

Eldorado Mountain Yoga Ashram
PO Box 307
Eldorado Springs, CO 80025
(303) 494-3051
email: eldo@sgry.org
web site: http://www.sgry.org/eldo

Shambhava School of Yoga-Denver
1553 Platte St., Ste 104
Denver, CO 80202
Contact: Sarah Simpson
(303) 758-0664
email: denver@sgry.org
web site:
http://www.sgry.org/denver

Shambhava School of Yoga-Grand Junction
PO Box 2632
Grand Junction, CO 81502
(970) 523-7248
Contact: Tom Tompkins
email: PVHZ65A@prodigy.com

Shambhava School of Yoga-Glenwood Springs
PO Box 1509
Glenwood Springs, CO 81602
(970) 945-2911
Contact: Anandi Jaffe
email: Nandi@sopris.net

Shambhava Arts
840 W. Dana St.
Mountain View, CA 94041
(650) 967-2210
Contact: Ashok & Lynn Srivastava
email:
meditation@worldnet.att.net
web site:
http://www.aspenleaf.com/meditation

Shambhava School of Yoga
Chidaksh Ashram
6 Slape Cresc
Burnside SA 5066
Australia
08-8271-1851
Contact: Peter & Rudrani Tooth
email:
Shambhava@camtech.net.au

1216 Harvey St.
McAllen, TX 78501
(956) 631-5309
Contact: Bob Carter
email: bobgraphic@aol.com

The 3rd House
Westbourne Rd.
Coltishall
Norfolk NR12 7HT
England
(0603)737933
Contact: Jess Hare
email: ganesh@zetnet.co.uk

Hawaii Center
PO Box 391015
Kailua Kona, HI 96739

S G R Y